What I Learned Today

Rikki Beadle-Blair

Published by Team Angelica Publishing 2011
an imprint of Angelica Entertainments Ltd

Team Angelica Publishing
51 Coningham Road
London W12 8BS

www.teamangelica.com

A CIP catalogue record for this book is available from the
British Library.

ISBN 978-0-95697-19-0-6

Printed and bound by Lightning Source.

About the author

Rikki Beadle-Blair was born and raised in South London. He attended the Bermondsey Lampost Free School where he could study whatever he liked and so focused on the arts and entertainment. He makes films, theatre, music, dance and art. His production company Team Angelica has developed several plays and films, including 'Bashment', 'Fit', 'KickOff', 'Taken In' and the South London Passion Plays. Passionate about encouraging creativity and self-expression, Rikki has developed several courses under the 'In the Room' banner to facilitate creative career advancement.

For all my friends

Thank you

I always wanted to keep a diary. I'd try for a few weeks, but so much happens in a day, it would always take over an hour each night to get it all down – an hour I could be spending on creating rather than rehashing. I wasn't sure of what it was I felt this vague duty to record anyway. Why would anyone ever want to know the details of my day? Why would I? When the day is done, it's done and gone – all that remains of value is what we've learned. ...Oh! *That's* what I wanted to make a record of – the current extra-steep learning curve of my life. I was in a particularly exciting period – our company was expanding, I was travelling lots, plus running my 'In the Room' courses and my weekly 'Career Clinic'. As I approached my 49th birthday and 50th year, I felt more wide-eyed than ever - I was learning so much - about business, creativity, work ethic and human behaviour. I wanted to learn these lessons thoroughly. I needed to take study-notes. So I started writing in my journal 'What I learned today' and making lists. *This* felt closer to right.

In the summer of 2011, I found myself in San Francisco, communicating with my London friends and co-workers via the internet. Facebook had just taken away the status update headline '*Rikki Beadle-Blair is...*' that each user would complete according to their mood. Now there was a blank space with the question: 'What's on your mind?' And so, fresh from my journal work, I answered the question and wrote 'What I learned today...' It felt good. So the next night I did it again - 'What I learned today #2': and then I was hooked.

Oddly, I quickly came to like the length limitation (422 characters including spaces). It forced me to focus my mind and pay closer attention to the nuance and texture of every word. Even though it might take up to an hour to hone each thought and encapsulate the day's lesson in a paragraph it never felt like time wasted. It became a sort of meditation – a lesson more deeply learned. So I kept going.

I thought I might drop it when I got home back home to London, or perhaps when I reached twenty-five or fifty...

I didn't think many people were actually bothering to read my statuses – maybe five or six friends a day? When I started getting 'likes' I was taken aback. And then over the next couple of months I started bumping into random people around town, around the country, and then around the world, who'd tell me that they were reading them regularly. By the time I reached #50, people were asking me to email them backdated statuses and whether I was going to compile them into a book. So when John Gordon and I started to talk seriously about Team Angelica going into publishing (initially to publish scripts from our new writing festivals) 'What I Learned Today' seemed like an obvious first choice.

So here it is. A year's worth of What I Learned Today. I realise that some of these ideas will not work for everyone – these are lessons that I have learned, not rules I insist others must follow. They are offerings not demands. Some of these thoughts have led to some spirited Facebook spats (#40 was the first to cause drama), so let it be said: None of these thoughts are intended as judgements on others. I understand that children and people with mental illnesses are not in the same position as the rest of us and that (for various reasons - including the possibility that they may just be wrong) many will struggle with these ideas – I certainly do myself. I do not live a perfectly balanced internal Zen existence and probably never will - but through these realisations and personal epiphanies I certainly live better. Happier. Stronger. Freer. More awake. More alive. And as long as I continue to open my mind to the lessons that the world brings me every day I know I can only continue to grow. In fact I can't wait to read these all again, unpack them, go deeper with them, act on them and continue to discuss them. Because I love to learn. Learning Is life.

I believe we all deserve to be free.

And the fact is that we are each of us responsible for our freedom.

This is not about letting others get away with anything. This is about understanding that no matter what others do - we own our responses, our moods and our lives.

This is about self-determination, but not selfishness.

Freeing ourselves and freeing others need to go in hand in hand – one does not work without the other.

That is what I have learned – and what I'm still learning.

I know these are not particularly original thoughts. But they were lightbulb moments for me and I want to share the light.

These thoughts are based in reality.

These thoughts have given me strength.

The core understanding inside them is simple:

Life is amazing and worthwhile - but life takes work.

We are amazing and worthwhile - and we take work too.

And the work is as follows…

What I learned today #1

To welcome this breath that passes through me and use it to live as fully and usefully and vibrantly as I can. Not later in the illusion we call the future - but right now, in This. Moment. This perfect moment - the greatest educator I will ever have: the only real moment there is ever is, was or will be. This moment right now is an epic romance... and I surrender myself to Life and Love.

What I learned today #2

To give up waiting. Waiting is a betrayal of the present moment, which is filled with all the magic, opportunity, joy and satisfaction any one person could ever need or handle. I am free and ready to make the most of every offer that each future event brings my way - but I need not wait. Life is not coming... life is Here. And life is more than enough to fill me to the brim...

What I learned today #3

Controlling others is a way of avoiding controlling yourself. What are you doing about the situation? What are you doing with your time? What are you focusing on? What's your contribution beyond criticism of others? Make sure you are meeting your own standards before setting them for others. Be your own living example.

What I learned today #4

Networking is not crawling or begging, it's taking an interest in people and making new friends. If you turn up with a begging bowl, you will feel like a pauper – so arrive bearing the riches of your abilities and talents and offer them to those who need them. That's the job. Reach out. Communicate. Connect. That's Art.

What I learned today #5

Learn your craft. Whether it's your art, your business, your home, philosophy or presentation skills. Study, observe, absorb - become an expert in your field. Read, watch, listen, dissect. Steal from the best, expand your vocabulary, learn your scales. Put it in your blender; develop own your creative recipe, keep growing, keep going.

What I learned today #6

To read mails and messages PROPERLY! The ones we receive and the ones we send. Proof-reading is KEY. As is staying calm and centred – do you actually need to send that angry email? Are you projecting a tone onto that text that was never there? Communication requires a cool head.

Rikki Beadle-Blair

What I learned today #7

The greatest teachers are the ones who are still excited about learning themselves. Great teachers are true diamonds that should be treasured. They understand that sometimes the problem child in the class is the secret genius. They know that given inspiration and stimulation, all of us are ravenous to learn. That they can learn from teaching us. They are us.

What I learned today #8

All you need is warm sun, cool water and laughing friends to feel forever young. Pack a picnic, book a trip, call up, drop round and rejuvenate. We are never lovelier than in the company of those we love.

Rikki Beadle-Blair

What I learned today #9

Conventional masculinity is great - but other versions have a lot to offer too. Just as classic femininity is a wonderful thing, but there are also other ways to be lovely. Instead of contemplating only one of two options for what makes us acceptable, why not offer ourselves to the world as we are – two billion individual role-models - each in our own way as delicate and strong as anyone needs to be?

What I learned today #10

That it is not humble for the heart to ask for less than it desires.... or to accept less than you deserve. It's okay to want, especially when it inspires those around to give. When the fruits of endeavour are shared, ambition can be an act of spectacular gratitude. Be generous and ask for the world.

Rikki Beadle-Blair

What I learned today #11

Empathy is the key to education. See a little of yourself in the face and fidgets of a child and perhaps he or she will see their face in you. Replace judgement with self-assessment and there is a chance for all of us to learn.

What I learned today #12

Anyone who is thwarting your progress is strengthening your process. Be grateful. Face your detractors and their demons and smile a silent thank you for their raising of the bar.

Rikki Beadle-Blair

What I learned today #13

Sometimes you have to bring your own sunshine.

What I learned today #14

The real secret to youth and beauty is a confident smile and that lil' snap in your step that announces: 'I've got it going on.' What can be sexier than a little gentle self-belief? Except perhaps a passionate belief in others? Make others feel young and sexy and you will be youth and sex itself – let them know we're good enough.

Rikki Beadle-Blair

What I learned today #15

Sometimes you simply have to relax and be the kid you really are; forget about what the world thinks of you or what you think of the world, just be in it and allow yourself to have some simple silly agenda-free fun with friends. You need to be a child if you want to keep growing.

What I learned today #16

Everyone needs acknowledgement, to feel significant; to feel valued; to feel loved. So often the greatest gift you can give and the greatest privilege you can receive - is to be there and listen.

Rikki Beadle-Blair

What I learned today #17

There is no better place than here - there is no better time than now. This moment is overflowing with opportunities. Wherever you want to go, you're going to have to get there from here. Whatever you want to do with your life, you are welcome to do it now. If you are wasting this moment, what is the point of hoping for more?

What I learned today (again) #18

Knowledge is not power. Knowledge is strength. Power over others is not strength. Vulnerability before others is strength. Knowledge does not lead to change - understanding does. Understanding is freedom. Wisdom is knowing when to be generous and when to be firm. Love is not power over others. Love is power surrendered, love is power shared.

Rikki Beadle-Blair

What I learned today #19

No possession is ever truly lost... it's exchanged; traded for experience, education, perspective, opportunity, or - best of all – freedom.

What I learned today #20

People are at their most aggressive when they are fearful. People are at their most fearful when they fear being insignificant. When we feel under attack is when we need to strive to be our most understanding, gracious, giving, gentle, clear, loving, firm and strong.

Rikki Beadle-Blair

What I learned today #21

There's no such thing as a true grown-up. Just adult behaviour. We never stop growing. And we never should. Life is growth, survival is change. Stay wide-eyed, gather wisdom, gain experience. Look into the mirror each day, explore your mind – and watch yourself unfold.

What I learned today #22

To be yourself in a culture of fearful conformism is a revolutionary act. To live in freedom and truth is a valentine to the world, a beautiful insurrection. Don't be afraid. Have the courage to aspire to more than acceptance. Aim for authenticity. You can scrub up, you can educate yourself, you can advance. But remember that, whatever you become, what you're starting with is already glorious.

Rikki Beadle-Blair

What I learned today #23

Once you are truly comfortable with yourself, you need never feel lonely. You are an essential part of every-thing - without your contribution the universe would be incomplete. We are all made of the same stuff - each connected to each - and can never be alone. Loneliness is a lie. We all belong - we all fit. So you might as well get comfortable and make yourself at home.

What I learned today #24

You cannot be a revolutionary and be loved by the regime - so do your thing without fear or shame or hungering for approval. The pursuit of acceptance can be a debilitating drug. Integrity and truth bring clarity. Have the strength and courage to be occasionally loathed and make your contribution.

Rikki Beadle-Blair

What I learned today #25

Never wish something easier - wish it harder, so you can get better and do it anyway. You don't get stronger by lifting lighter and lighter weights. You don't get faster by skipping the training. Seek out challenges, welcome them, get stronger.

What I learned today #26

There is no greater opportunity than an empty canvas.

Rikki Beadle-Blair

What I learned today #27

To give up the concept of 'hard work'. It's not about work - it's about total involvement. Giving yourself entirely in every way to your passion and vision. As Bruce Lee said 'Become water', flexible, powerful, essential - and pouring yourself into the great big everything- every drop of one's being. This is fulfilment.

What I learned today #28

Forget what I want from life - what does life want from me? What do I have to offer? What does the world need and cry out for? I think about that and everything falls into place: what to wear, what to say, what to communicate and create, and how to conduct myself as I do it. ... It's not about me – It's about us. Ask for nothing - offer everything.

Rikki Beadle-Blair

What I learned today #29

Pursue passion, and the years will fly but you will never feel old. I wake vibrating, awaiting the lessons of today, as rashly infatuated as a child, still fascinated and moved by our humanity - deeply inspired and utterly convinced I must do all I was born to; leaving heart-shaped footprints as I run the pavements, sands, tundras, valleys and bridges of this dazzling mysterious world.

What I learned today #30

Years cannot age us. Fear can frustrate us - disappointment can distract us - bitterness can block and break us - but take a real big bite out of this ripening life, let the juice drip down your chin, and who can stop themselves from beaming like a child? Survival is victory - the higher the number the higher the score. We're winning.

Rikki Beadle-Blair

What I learned today #31

This breath right here is life. Our acceptance of right now is the key living. This existence is opportunity in abundance. How we spend it is the truth and the proof of who we choose to be.

What I learned today #32

People only inflict hurt to try and heal themselves. It doesn't work, it just distributes the hurt. So before I take revenge I ask: will this heal or mutate my pain into a disease? Reduce life or expand it? Bring energy or drain it away? Is this my best offering to the world? Then do what makes me the most fabulous and find the grace and courage to thank my enemy for the opportunity.

Rikki Beadle-Blair

What I learned today #33

There are no endings, only beginnings. There is no death, just transformation. There are no failures, just results. There are no disappointments, just un-met expectations. There are no disasters, only opportunities.

What I learned today #34

When your life turns into horror movie listen carefully to your own voice: is the maniac calling you from inside the house?

Rikki Beadle-Blair

What I learned today #35

To take anything for granted is to render it invisible - the little death that makes us killers. Why save all our thank-yous for compliments from strangers while greeting mum's phone-calls and kisses with sighs? Craning for a glimpse of a shooting star while crushing countless glittering blades of dewy grass with each oblivious step. It's not what we own that makes us rich. It's what we value.

What I learned today #36

Labelling is a lazy and a lie. Calling ourselves black/white/yellow/brown/gay/straight/bi, young/old /mid-life, good/evil, even male/female, is like glancing at the sky and only seeing stars where there are planets, suns, solar systems, comets and galaxies. Building boxes for each other builds cells for our potential, as our complexity - both shared and individual - is incarcerated.

Rikki Beadle-Blair

What I learned today #37

Competition with others is self-defeating. Comparison with others is a waste of your gifts. Envy is a tragedy. There never has been, and never will be again, anyone like you; those who fail to appreciate you are missing out on the miracle. So appreciate yourself: your beauty and brilliance. Run your own race and bring home the gold – which is life fully lived. This is our contribution to creation.

What I learned today #38

To take responsibility. The question is not, 'Why are they doing this to me?' but, why am I doing this to me? Moreover, why am I doing this to them? Saddling other poor souls with the power to render me frustrated or fulfilled; planting the keys for my happiness in their back pocket when I am the sole architect and builder of my world, too lazy to be its caretaker.

Rikki Beadle-Blair

What I learned today #39

No more 'Why me?' Why NOT me? Who made this life and these choices? Who is open and ready to take on these challenges and thrive? Hungry to make a real contribution employing the fruits of my education? Strong enough to face this world without fear and celebrate each opportunity for deeper understanding. Me, of course. Why not me? Try me, teach me, humble me, empower me. Bring it on.

What I learned today #40

Forgiveness is arrogance. It's not our place to forgive others - they have done nothing wrong, they are merely doing what they hope will make them feel better - as they should, however cruel or oblivious their actions seem to us. It's now our turn to make ourselves happy - by employing understanding, acceptance, affection, honesty, generosity and sometimes by simply letting go and moving on.

Rikki Beadle-Blair

What I learned today #41

Creativity is rebirth. A daily resurrection from the ashes of my ego - shot down in flames by the knowledge that I still have so far to go. But imagine if I'd learned everything, achieved everything, was loved and lauded by all and could do no wrong? My journey complete? No... that would be a melancholy kind of death: the child in me that still loves to learn prefers life – in all its perfect imperfection. Let life criticize me, let life challenge me. Let life teach me – to live.

What I learned today #42

Energy is key. Sourcing it, creating it, expending, receiving, sharing it. The stingier we are with our energy the less life gives us back. Flow is the goal and the way we live each moment determines that flow. What we eat, what we do, how we treat and respond to others, what we demand from life and ourselves. What we pursue, think about, say, choose to focus on and offer. We are energy.

Rikki Beadle-Blair

What I learned today #43

Rejection by others is an invitation to accept them and their right to their opinions and decisions; accept the offer to turn your light up brighter and reveal who you really are - someone who accepts him/herself, celebrates their being and shares their spirit with those who are ready to benefit from their bounty. Rejection is a chance to get strong, do your thing anyway and be free.

What I learned today #44

Judgment of others is autobiography; revealing so much more about me than the other person. The next time I criticize or categorize others I can take the opportunity to interrogate my own thoughts and projections and ask myself, what does this opinion say about me? How can I expand beyond my limited perspective and superficial view of others? How can I see us both more clearly?

Rikki Beadle-Blair

What I learned today #45

Ownership is an illusion, which, when we grip an item too tightly, becomes a delusion, creating suffering as we place our worth in identifying with objects. One day all things will disintegrate and move on to serve another purpose, as will we. Why feel loss when we can celebrate the eternal journey of all things? All that can be truly possessed by us is our soul... and why not share that too?

What I learned today #46

Our only obstacle is our unwillingness to take action. Our only limitation the boundaries of our determination. Our ability is never seriously in question, only our passion. Hesitation is a sign that you are not in love; when we pursue what we truly love we are unstoppable.

Rikki Beadle-Blair

What I learned today #47

Why waste time wishing you had someone else's face, when you already have more beauty than you are able to appreciate? Surrender to your beauty and your brilliance - give your life to making the most of it and you will light up the world. All living things head towards the light – all you have to do is shine.

What I learned today #48

To love the rain - which some living thing elsewhere is craving while I complain. Rain is life. As it beats you back, it offers you the chance to recognise this proof that you're heading somewhere you really want to go and that you cannot be stopped. Suffering is created when we wish for sunshine, blind to this perfect moment we're in. Embrace all weathers: feel the rain kiss your face and know you're alive.

Rikki Beadle-Blair

What I learned today #49

That rest is as crucial to progress as effort. To inhale you must exhale, to journey you need to refuel, to be fully awake you must sleep. So good to switch off that phone and sprawl out in the long grass for a long lazy moment, stretch your spine and close your eyes and let the Earth do the spinning. And then dive back into the water refreshed, repaired and ready.

What I learned today #50

Guilt is a frozen dead burdensome emotion unless it is alchemized into action and our missteps inspire us to do better, live better, love better. Why be dull suffering gravestones to our past ignorance when we can be living, gleaming monuments to those we have wronged or lost and the lessons they have taught us? Guilt is a tiny seed – let's be trees, bearing grateful blossoms of experience.

Rikki Beadle-Blair

What I learned today #51

Feeling is not enough. What are you doing with this emotion? Are you using it to stay stuck in a moment? Or to fire you forward into the next adventure? We can still respect our feelings while assessing them - Too cocky? Self-pity? Ego spiralling? The event you're reacting to is already over - are you focusing on responses that make this new moment the best it can be?

What I learned today #52

You cannot save everyone. People deserve the right to ignore you just as you dismissed warning signs on your own journey to wisdom. No one has a duty to remain unscathed just to please you. You can only help those are ready - but you can love everyone and judge no one and take the opportunity to replace the words 'I told you so' with your silent open arms.

Rikki Beadle-Blair

What I learned today #53

Dreams are for the dreaming - visions are for visionaries. It's never too late to dedicate yourself to getting lightning-clear about your passions, your capabilities and your purpose; to waking every day and staying awake: taking each step with clarity and certainty; giving yourself over to a life that fills you to brimming; to becoming decisively entirely alive.

What I learned today #54

We are all teachers. We teach others how to treat us, how to behave around us, what they can get away with, what our buttons are, how to hurt us. So we can also teach others how to love us; not just by loving ourselves, or loving them - but by loving everything. Teach others how to respect us by respecting everything. Show them how to value us by valuing everything - and everyone - we know.

Rikki Beadle-Blair

What I learned today #55

Only one person can truly deeply hurt us: ourselves. Pain can be inflicted but suffering is entirely self-manufactured and self-maintained. What if we decided there would be no suffering today? What if we just refused to be wounded and experienced everything as a welcome sensation? How much more time would we find to get things done? How much time would become free for us to simply live?

What I learned today #56

So many plans to save the world - so many worthwhile ambitions - yet none greater or more challenging than being where you are - fully present and able to appreciate yourself, look after yourself, make peace with yourself. Achieve that and with this first miracle - this act of salvation - the real work has begun. Living each second of existence fully and consciously... is true ambition.

Rikki Beadle-Blair

What I learned today #57

To let today be an adventure, encourage tomorrow to be interesting, and ensure that yesterday was worthwhile. My arms are open.

What I learned today #58

To seek out loving criticism and use it gratefully to get better, stronger, braver, clearer in intent - whether in agreement or defiance. It is fuel, it is food and the thing that all creatures crave - attention. So I vow to open my mind and consume critique. Breathe it in, calm my ego, give thanks and employ this chance to dig deeper and give more to each new creative adventure.

Rikki Beadle-Blair

What I learned today #59

That all limitations are a gift encouraging your creativity, your resourcefulness, your determination. Even death reminds you that all you have - this breath, this moment, this life - is precious, and you'd better make the most of it. No friction, no fire. If there was no gravity we'd just float away with no control – it's because of gravity we build wings.

What I learned today #60

No one can be everywhere every second and be everything to everyone. Emails fall through the cracks, phone-calls get missed, the ball gets dropped, the spinning plates go crashing. You can't be loved every second by everyone. You can stay calm, clear and centred and love everyone from where you are. There is always time for love. Admit you're human. Pick up the ball. Relax. Refocus. Resume. Love.

Rikki Beadle-Blair

What I learned today #61

People tell you all you need to know the first day you meet them: their issues, dramas, weaknesses and flaws are all up front, hiding in throwaway comments ("My friends say I'm a liar/playa/slacker/thief...") lurking in self-deprecating jokes or spelt out in blatant confessions or actions that you choose to dismiss. Folks love to confess to strangers. You are being warned - are you listening?

What I learned today #62

When someone says they are not in love with you - dumps you, fires you, expels you - be thankful. They are doing you a favour. Instead of wasting your time and quietly insulting you with tepid semi-commitment and a roving eye, they are setting you free to find love with someone appreciative and willing. At least they love you that much. Love them in return and release both of you. That's love.

Rikki Beadle-Blair

What I learned today #63

Worry is a waste of vital energy that could be channelled into doing what needs to be done. And if you can't do it, never be too proud to ask someone who can. Are we ever actually helpless? Or just hopeless? Worrying is wanking. Fix it or forget it.

What I learned today #64

There is no better weather than this weather; no more fun to be had; no better life to be led than this. No better tomorrow. There is only this perfect second right here and all it takes for this to be the best period in my life is for me to open my eyes, heart and mind, accept it for all it is and move forward from here... To the next perfect second. All this magic time is waiting for - is appreciation.

Rikki Beadle-Blair

What I learned today #65

People cannot lie. They will try - and they will sometimes seem to succeed in fooling us for a while - but
there is always a clue - a twitch, a 'tell', a disguised
confession. And then it's our turn as we habitually
attempt to lie to ourselves, aiding and abetting our
desperate deceivers. But the truth is always there
calling out to be heard. Are you listening?

What I learned today #66

Take compliments without resistance. Why rob others
of the chance to show fondness and appreciation and
yourself of encouragement? Why let ego drama hijack a
simple instance of connection? If you feel their words
are insincere and undeserved you can be sincere in
your efforts to live up to them. Welcome compliments
and return the gift. Stay humble and be fabulous.

Rikki Beadle-Blair

What I learned today #67

To say I Love You. All around us people are craving our love and hungry to hear it spoken. If we find it hard to say, all the more reason to give in and gain some release. So we might sound soft? Soft is the new strong. So our parents, siblings, friends, lovers, exes, enemies and crushes might think we're crazy? Crazy is witholding love in a world that needs it so badly. Speak up. Speak Love.

What I learned today #68

Sometimes the kindest, most helpful thing you can say is No. Trying to please everyone is an impossible juggle, and sometimes people hate you if you give them everything they want anyway. So if you're not sure and you can't commit your time/money/attention/ involvement without reservation or resentment, just giving a calm respectful No can free everyone involved.

Rikki Beadle-Blair

What I learned today #69

Let go of home clutter. Stuff you don't use, don't need, slows you down. Make a home that inspires clarity, an oasis from the hustle, a launch-pad for your ambitions; a safe house that opens its arms to all who set foot in it. Then get out in the field to pursue your passions and earn your return, falling spent and happy into your home's embrace.

What I learned today #70

Let go of clothing clutter. Get rid of any clothes that don't fit you, don't flatter you or fail to represent you. You may have many images, many flavours, but make sure they are all a true aspect of you. Never leave the house looking or feeling less than a star - for that is what you are.

Rikki Beadle-Blair

What I learned today #71

Let go of admin clutter - unpaid bills, unanswered emails, unopened letters, unfinished accounts, incomplete taxes. Face it all, tackle the debts and conquer the stress; clear the desk and your worries so you can move forward with a lighter mind and your head out of the sand; get on top of your business; become free to focus on what matters. Free.

#What I learned today #72

Let go of emotional clutter - grievances and grudges that keep you mired and disempowered; crippling bitterness that renders you small and petty - missing out on this invaluable education that could make you a graceful giant of humanity. Let go of the lazy blaming that hands your power to those who cannot carry it and take hold of your own glorious existence.

Rikki Beadle-Blair

What I learned today #73

Never act out of anger; you'll always snatch at short-term solutions and send all long-term benefits to Hell along with any lasting peace. Rage is an intoxicant - clouding perception, warping ego and blurring judgment; addictive, corrosive, ultimately destructive. Save that furious text/email for the morning, then press send or delete with a clear head and sure vision of what you need to achieve.

What I learned today #74

Never make a fear-based decision. It's always wise and practical to choose self-preservation - but holding back from exploration, creativity, expansion and freedom, reveals fear as the thief of life. If it's failure or criticism you fear, then go ahead and try it anyway, wear it anyway, say it anyway, express yourself anyway, love anyway, be yourself anyway. Be the lion you are and live your life.

Rikki Beadle-Blair

What I learned today #75

There's no shame is accepting offers of help - sharing your vulnerability and humanity can be a gift to friends and family. Be generous to those that need you to need them sometimes. Respect your imperfect humanity and honour your place in the human chain. Give yourself the opportunity to marvel at the kindness of others and offer your gratitude in exchange.

What I learned today #76

To be loved by everyone is not possible or desirable. To learn grace you must take some tumbles, to take flight you must ruffle some feathers and to be truly generous, you must give others license to hate you, get competitive with you, misunderstand you, misrepresent you, hurt you a little and (gasp) ignore you! You can't demand to receive universal love, but you can offer it. To everyone.

Rikki Beadle-Blair

What I learned today #77

Stop wanting what's on the other person's plate - fruitlessly yearning for other lives to distract you from taking responsibility for the choices you've made and the life you've created. Family, friends, neighbours and workmates are only delivering what you've told them you'll accept. Appreciate their efficiency and eat what you've ordered or order something else.

What I learned today #78

The characteristics you suspect hold you back - your background, your build, your face, your style - are what will take you forward. That's your gimmick – that's your speciality. Attached to every label is a key that fits your fast car to creativity, fulfilment, freedom. Own who you are. Turn the label over and find yourself written there. Enjoy yourself and make the most of yourself. Be Superyou.

Rikki Beadle-Blair

What I learned today #79

Our beauty and our strength is in our diversity, collectively and individually. Smart and stupid, cynical and naive, private and exhibitionistic, sophisticated but council estate, masculine/feminine, gentle yet sturdy, fearless and shy - I am too many colours for one brush, too many flavours for one spoon, too many shots for one target. And I refuse to let a single amazing atom go to waste.

What I learned today #80

The best way to get appreciation is to give it. Give respect to critics and turn them into trainers - rivals into sparring partners. Anyone who opposes you is giving you valuable energy. Take all intended negativity, flow with it, convert it into fuel and take off. Face stupidity and seize the invitation to education. Lesson One: The best way to dispose of our enemies is to turn them into friends.

Rikki Beadle-Blair

What I learned today #81

Whatever you truly want, you must become. You want a great lover? Be a great lover. Want to work? Provide work. You hunger to conquer showbiz? Be Showbiz - as glamorous, powerful and credible as you perceive it to be - with your unique flavour added. Looking for inspiration? So is everyone - especially in Showbusiness. Be the business – and the business will come to you.

What I learned today #82

Focus is food. What you focus on thrives and grows like a child you carry in your belly. Focus on what you don't have and the emptiness at your core will expand until it swallows you, however many possessions you accumulate. In fact the more you buy, the poorer you'll be. Focus on what you have- relish it, luxuriate in it, make the most of it ...and watch as your riches grow.

Rikki Beadle-Blair

What I learned today #83

Gratitude makes us millionaires. Everything in your life is a gift. Everyone you meet, every challenge that's offered to you. Your day is filled with opportunities: to learn, to adapt, to strengthen, to flow, to grow. Every breath is a miracle and a testament to your survival. Show appreciation and watch your life appreciate in return. Get richer with every thank you that you say and feel.

What I learned today #84

False modesty serves no one. The world needs our naked ambition - courageous pioneers taking reckless strides into the wilderness, conquering oceans, discovering new continents, dissolving frontiers. When we abandon our timid dreams to pursue our visions and seize this one life, we truly help make this world all it can be. Richer, brighter, kinder, braver, beautiful - alive.

Rikki Beadle-Blair

What I learned today #85

There are no disasters – only opportunities. Who we are is revealed by our response to the unexpected, the unfair, the unplanned. That moment when it all falls apart heralds your shining time to pull it all together, scoop up the wreckage and make great art. Are you willing to seize this offer to rebuild, restart, rethink, reconstitute, be reborn? Are you ready to be extraordinary?

What I learned today #86

We have no enemies, only saviours. Every opponent is a teacher, every attack an education, every obstacle a call for the spirit to triumph. Those who betray you are building your independence, those who doubt you are throwing down a gauntlet, daring you to become even more determined to manifest your intent and fulfil your life's purpose. Salute them, value them, defy them and inspire the world.

Rikki Beadle-Blair

What I learned today #87

Lying is a sign of dissatisfaction; an admission we're not happy with how things are - our age, history, status and achievements. If you cannot be proud of your circumstances then something needs to be either changed or accepted. And if you catch someone in a lie, you are witnessing a form of panic. Is it time for compassion? Do you really need to make them any unhappier than they already are?

What I learned today #88

When someone's desperate enough to lie about us, we can get distracted by ego - obsessing on how we're seen by others - or we can simply stay focused on truth. Is there any truth in what's been said? Does it matter what people think of us? Does the truth need to be told or will it tell itself through how we live our lives? Time spent judging others (even liars) can be a missed opportunity to know ourselves.

Rikki Beadle-Blair

What I learned today #89

Defence is an act of war. Resistance feeds the battle. It's not our place to demand that others be civil, truthful or open-minded, but to be respectful to our own morality and offer what we demand. If we want acceptance, why not accept the other's lack of it? If we hunger for understanding, why not understand their ignorance? It's not 'How dare they?' but 'Why dare they?' Understanding is grace.

What I learned today #90

It's our duty to be sexy. We're in this world for love; some to procreate and all to inspire it. When we assert our sensuality and beauty, we encourage others to do the same. Don't take lovers for granted - consecrate your union with constant kisses. If you're single, roll in your sheets and strut down the streets, celebrating your perfection and dazzling contribution to this spectacular world.

Rikki Beadle-Blair

What I learned today #91

When you eat more than you'd meant to, drink more than you need, spend more than you can afford, something in you is pleading for a conversation. Obesity is a sign of undernourishment, the body calling out 'more, more', hoping to siphon grains of goodness from processed food. Next time you over-indulge in any area, don't punish yourself, ask yourself, 'What am I really hungry for?'

What I learned today #92

Your body is your best friend; a home constructed of miracles for your soul to live in; loyal and unfailingly honest with you about the consequences of your lifestyle and the adjustments you need to make to survive. And do you repay it with appreciation and acceptance? Or with frustration, criticism, punishment and neglect? Listen to your buddy and be grateful. Be loving to your body and be kind.

Rikki Beadle-Blair

What I learned today #93

Whenever I'm unsure of what to say, what to do, what to eat, where to turn, how to respond, pick myself up, free myself, cleanse myself, rise above, go forward - Live with a capital L - there's only one moral question I need to ask myself: What will make me the best I can be? However narrow the options seem, there's always at least one offer on the table – the chance to be fabulous.

What I learned today #94

When I'm looking for inspiration, I think back to the old neighbourhood and the kid who knew exactly who he was, what he was worth and what he wanted - before he was sold the lie that he didn't belong 'cause he didn't look, talk, walk, think, act or dream like the others - and I'm beautiful again... Bright again. I'm me again, young and free and fearless and I know exactly what to do. And I do it.

Rikki Beadle-Blair

What I learned today #95

You don't need permission to be an artist - and certainly not to be yourself. Why burden others with the need for their approval? The world is hungry for fresh bold ideas and that is what you are: a dazzling one-off experiment, unique; incomparable; invaluable. Do your thing, do it today and do it your own way, employing your own brand of fearless grace. The world is waiting.

What I learned today #96

Everyone needs some time with themselves to take stock and get clear on what they need, want and have. Every now and then we all need to go back to our heartbeat and find our rhythm and march forward to the beat of our drum. Calm brings clarity, clarity brings confidence , confidence brings creativity. And creativity is life.

Rikki Beadle-Blair

What I learned today #97

The truth is never to be feared. As long as we keep sight of who we are and where we're heading, nothing can shake us off course, certainly not the facts. An opinion is not a truth beyond the fact that someone holds it - and we can cope with that. Whatever life throws at us, we can absorb and learn from. Not everything that can be faced can be fixed - but nothing can be fixed unless it is faced.

What I learned today #98

There are so many things worth working for beyond money - truth, joy, enlightenment, advancement, freedom. Money offers advantages, but it is not freedom - who could be more bitter and frustrated than a slave wearing a chain made of gold? The spirit it takes to have as much adventure with a penny as a pound, now that's worth working for. I refuse to simply make a living, when I can make a life.

Rikki Beadle-Blair

What I learned today #99

Everyone is hungering for the same thing - connection - the proof that we matter - that we are matter - that we are here, and that someone cares. It's my purpose to let everyone I meet know that I see them, hear them, feel them. That I am glad they are here and that I am here with them. That no matter who they are or what they have done - they belong... that they are loved.

What I learned today #100

I've never met anyone who could not be a star. Every one of us is capable of becoming a legend if we want to, whatever our background or our appearance. The key is to embrace who you are, including your 'flaws' and present yourself within the correct context with commitment and authenticity. It entails sacrifice and demands vision, but find the right vehicle and audience and there you are: shining.

Rikki Beadle-Blair

What I learned today #101

Never feel sorry for yourself for more than an hour.
Feel the wound, the shock, the bitterness, then remember: if suffering is entirely self-created and maintained, that is a position of power. Recovery is in your power. Put aside your disappointment (that's all it ever is) and look for the offer. Even in the darkest hour there's always an offer. Consider it and you reclaim control - and the key to progress.

What I learned today #102

Everything is perfect; each reaction the perfect logical result of a previous action. Consequence is never coincidence. If we want better we must do better. If we want to feel better in the future we must respond better to what's taking place now - this response is instigating what occurs next. When we desire change, the starting place is never outside us. It is right here, right now, within us.

Rikki Beadle-Blair

What I learned today #103

To wish for what we don't possess is to insult what we have and miss who we are; a painful abuse of our abundance. We are already so rich compared to many - already famous in our circle, already blessed in our own way. If instead of hoping for charity we focus on expansion of our resources we will find all the riches we ever needed and the greatest treasure of all - independence.

What I learned today #104

Nothing can destroy us quicker than getting what we want when we are not ready for it. We have to find joy in the quest and not delay it until the conquest; to mine the pleasure that exists in this very instant - the only pleasure that's available, the only moment that actually exists. Tomorrow never comes, but that's okay: today is enough.

Rikki Beadle-Blair

What I learned today #105

Become what you crave. If you want a good friend, be one. If you want the milkmaid's milk, become a cow: she will notice you then. And when the milkmaid stops to make enquiries you can offer to compare flavours together and hey presto – there's your milk. And the best part is that you don't even need it now – 'cause you're the cow. The sole supplier of all your satisfaction.

What I learned today #106

Bad luck does not exist; just opportunity and the ability to identify and capitalize on it. We're all lucky every day - but rarely in ways that are anticipated or immediately convenient. Your life is working for you constantly. How greatly you benefit is almost entirely down to your willingness to let go of your expectations and welcome the wealth of available possibilities. Discount your deficits, be defined by your blessings.

Rikki Beadle-Blair

What I learned today #107

You are a success. If you're in the gutter hugging a bottle you are a successful drunk. If you're sitting at home hating your agent waiting for them to call with your big break you are an extremely successful unsuccessful actor. Are you identified with failure? Is your energy focus feeding what you don't want and don't have? Shift focus and change what you choose to be successful at.

What I learned today #108

Everyone fits. Each of us is an essential irreplaceable part of everything. Nothing ever dies. We feed each other's existence. I inhale your skin flakes, you breathe me in, and I fill your lungs as we exchange and interchange. There is no enemy, no one to judge. Separation is an illusion. We are made of the same stuff as the sand and sea. We are all miraculous. We are all stars.

Rikki Beadle-Blair

What I learned today #109

It's not about what I want from life, it's about what life wants from me. How can I best contribute? Be of service? When I am sharing all I have is when I feel my most fortunate; when I am giving all I've got is when I feel my most blessed. Nothing fills you up like purpose. Sate your appetite by cooking for others - quench your thirst by becoming the well.

What I learned today #110

We are living the life we have created. If we are in a trap, it has been built by following a blueprint we have designed. If we are disappointed, frustrated or lost, it is due to our own past and present failures to be grateful, courageous and focused. That can change right now, if we permit ourselves to inhale each breath of life and the countless exciting opportunities it offers us.

Rikki Beadle-Blair

What I learned today #111

The thought you're having right now is creating the world you are living in, defining this moment and designing your future. Who are you choosing to be? Blessed or cursed? A victim of an angry obstructive world or a pioneer on a frontier of challenges and adventures? Are you ready for the freedom that comes with taking total responsibility? It's time to let yourself be as fortunate as you are.

What I learned today #112

It's not the artist's job to express him or herself but OURself - the connections that exist between us all; the flaws and frailties we share as we share the same ancestor, the same humanity. To help those who feel outcast to know they belong; that this world and all it offers is owned by each of us. To show all who feel lonely that no one is ever alone: the air connects us.

Rikki Beadle-Blair

What I learned today #113

You cannot control anything or anyone, only influence them. Power over others or over life is an illusion that can only lead to a greater unquenchable sense of need. The only available hope for power is control over your own responses to life's evolving circumstances. Are you ready to gently seize each passing opportunity for grace and understanding? Are you ready to graze on truth and grow?

What I learned today #114

Surrender to your beauty. Comparing yourself to others in an unwinnable competition that is painful and pointless. Instead of resisting your appearance, why not glory in it? If you can't appreciate yourself, then asking anyone else to do it for you is lazy, arrogant and unreasonable. Look in the mirror without expectation or judgement and see yourself for the first time and watch beauty grow.

Rikki Beadle-Blair

What I learned today #115

Surrender to your individuality. Your own brand of masculine and feminine, traditionalist and maverick, child and parent, stereotype and contradiction. Make no apology for your unique blend of humanity, offer yourself with fearless humility. Let's forget acceptance from others and accept ourselves - passionately and whole-heartedly - inspiring all we meet to celebrate themselves in turn.

What I learned today #116

Surrender to your courage. Are you braver than you've allowed yourself to be? Is it time to pursue the vision of life you have suppressed and step off the conventional path? You don't have to earn meaningless money to impress others with success symbols that mean nothing, and you don't need to play Mr/Miss Ordinary while you ache for an epic existence. Be bold, be brave, be you.

Rikki Beadle-Blair

What I learned today #117

Surrender to your complexity. You don't always have to be right. You don't always need to be smart. You don't always want to be consistent. How would you gather wisdom if you were? While striving to become your best version of yourself, cut yourself some slack and celebrate your layers and levels, and allow your contradictions to teach you how to appreciate the complexity of others.

What I learned today #118

Surrender to your power. Nothing is more freeing than realising you're entirely responsible for the relationships you have, the home you have, the body you have, the career you have. We are entirely free to live the life we choose, and if we're unhappy or frustrated it's because we've chosen to be. You can change this world with one idea: the decision to live your authentic life... Ready?

Rikki Beadle-Blair

What I learned today #119

Surrender to your creativity. You need never be lost for ideas in this world - there is no excuse for being bored. If you feel cornered, be grateful for this motivation to venture off the beaten path. The adventure starts here within you - your spirit is all the motor that's needed; it will take you anywhere - and wherever you go with joy, passion and courage, the inspired world will follow.

What I learned today #120

Every day in so many ways we reject offers of love, turning down invites, ignoring calls, dodging lovers, shouting down family. How much love have we missed today? What would our lives be like if we only ever said yes to love? If we continually offered love to everyone we know, regardless of whether they deserve it? Now that's achievement: to become the well-spring of love.

Rikki Beadle-Blair

What I learned today #121

If there's a shortfall between what you want and what you have, ask yourself what is it you've not been willing to do? Looking at the great achievers - Ali, M.J., Shakespeare, Picasso - it was always about their work ethic: total sacrifice, zero compromise. It's never crowded on the extra mile: is that because you're not there? You have to give the life you have to get the life you want.

What I learned today #122

You can't rely on others to build your self-esteem, it's too much responsibility for anyone to bear and won't last - what's been given can be taken away. Do you find yourself sexy? Do you appreciate your beauty or brains? It's unreasonable to ask others to have more faith in you than you have yourself. If you want others to see your value, you need to lead the way. Appreciate yourself.

Rikki Beadle-Blair

What I learned today #123

Keep It Simple. Whether telling a story, creating art or music, devising a plan or schedule, or facing objections and angry opposition. Avoid complicated relationships and confusing interactions. Don't get involved in pointless politics and game-playing. Stop trashing valuable time trying to win or obsessing on being right. Trust the truth, stick to it, live it. Clarity is a gift to humanity.

What I learned today#124

There is no greater love than the love of this moment - where you are right now, who you are and who you're with. Let yourself fall head over heels in love with this breath you're taking, this lesson you're learning, these fruits of your labours and choices. This life you've made, like a child, needs attention and appreciation to flourish and grow.

Rikki Beadle-Blair

What I learned today #125

The only one who can set your limits is you. No one else can distract or thwart you. Obstacles exist only in your mind, fortified by your belief system. Challenges are merely there to make the quest more fun. Other people's scepticism or faith in you can be used either to paralyse or galvanize you - by you and only you, the holder to the keys, the CEO of your own business: Life Unlimited.

What I learned today #126

What you achieve is nothing compared to how you achieve it. Are you being your best self? Have you worked to contribute as much as you've worked to receive? Have you made those you've met or spoken to, those who've served you along with those who've liked, loved or supported you on your journey feel met, heard, served, supported and loved? Are you living the life the world deserves?

Rikki Beadle-Blair

What I learned today #127

I now know my calling - to be a resource, a place people can go to find themselves, know themselves, express themselves, develop themselves, explore themselves, fulfil themselves, love themselves, advance themselves, be themselves. Mentor, student, sibling, chronicler... a font of understanding... a friend. My calling is to be here for you.

What I learned today #128

Scarcity is not beauty. If we could appreciate the beauty in what we see every day - starting with ourselves - what kind of world would this be? It's not egotistical to be a beautiful part of a beautiful world – it's stingy to withhold and deny our contribution to this perfection. Release your loveliness and you coax the shy beauty out of everything and free somebody's fearful soul.

Rikki Beadle-Blair

What I learned today #129

Pretty is not beauty. Fashionable is not beauty. Popular is not beauty. Youth is not beauty. Beauty is that neon glow that lights you up on those random carefree occasions when you cease caring about what you think people are looking for and show them who you are: ageless, shameless, sexy, innocent, truthful, gentle, strong, loving, universal, unique and undiluted. Beauty is you. You are beauty.

What I learned today #130

Say thank you to your oppressors. The more daunting the challenge, the bigger the benefaction. This is not about free passes for bullies – it's about freeing you. Put down your grievances, your wounds and your hunger for retribution, and see how light and agile you become. Gratitude is the key to your mind-jail, thank you is a signal for a mass pardon - and you will be the first to be set free.

Rikki Beadle-Blair

What I learned today #131

Approval is a prison and I refuse to be chained. I will wear what I want, say I what I want, love who I want. I will work the way I want. My Life – my Art. I don't have to please anyone, and sure as heck can't please everyone. And if ever people wonder who the hell I think I am, one look at me and they'll know. 'Cause I was born free and I will live and die that way.

What I learned today #132

Whatever you create or achieve in your life, it's how you make people feel that will be remembered. Are you supportive, understanding, inspiring? Or manipulative, judgemental, needy? Do you bring energy to others or take it away? The truly great make others feel their greatness. Invest in everyone you meet and surround yourself with stars.

Rikki Beadle-Blair

What I learned today #133

You don't have to love yourself before you can love anyone else, you can love everything and everyone at the same time - including yourself. You are equal to everything else in creation, no better and no worse. All of us, whatever labels we've been given, are exactly the same. Made of the same matter as one another and the sun, sea, and sky. We are all of us stars walking on the earth.

What I learned today #134

Wherever you want to go, you can't get there from anywhere other than where you are, so what's the point of wishing for a different start? Enjoy your journey and envy no one. Choose your destination with your passion, not your fear. Everyone you encounter is here to help you in some way - nobody is your enemy, no one is your stepping stone. Arriving is a mere bonus if you make each step golden.

Rikki Beadle-Blair

What I learned today #135

When a stranger tells me I am going to Hell - for the life I'm leading, the work I do, the people I love - I'm not wounded. I understand now that it's not a condemnation, it's an invitation - to the Hell they live in, a place of anger and fear. So I smile... I lean towards understanding... and there it is... inside me. And there I am in Heaven - holding out my hand in invitation.

What I learned today #136

You cannot mend yourself by forcing others to take the cure. Our parents did the best they could within the limitations of their consciousness; our spouses are simply who they are: our dissatisfaction is the fruit of our own choices. The only way to get truly healthy is to take that long loving honest look in the mirror and do what's required. Heal ourselves and we heal our families. Save ourselves and we save the world.

Rikki Beadle-Blair

What I learned today #137

No one has power over us. Ever. They can restrain the body, wound, criticize, even destroy it; our body is a home worth inhabiting and protecting, but who we actually are is our spirit and free will. If we decide to do what others want in order to facilitate our life on earth, that's still a choice. We are free until our last breath, and pretending to ourselves that we are helpless traps us in a prison of alibis.

What I learned today #138

I refuse to be a cynic. I'm uninterested in being jaded or world-weary. I'm committed to being alive in every fibre of me, to my ongoing love affair with this breath-taking voyage of discovery and the boundless possibility that rises with each day and never sets. I believe in the wisdom of the elder and the wild spirit of the young. I believe in the expression of our evolving humanity. I believe in us.

Rikki Beadle-Blair

What I learned today #139

Honour where you came from, appreciate where you are, celebrate how you got here, claim where you are going. Enjoy your journey. And wherever you are at any point in time, make the most of it and you will make the most of yourself. You belong in this world. You are this world. Keep moving.

What I learned today #140

Sometimes you have to let people go on their journey and through their drama without you. Sometimes you have to let a loved one hate you. If you've always acted out of love, trust them to keep that memory somewhere behind their blinding suffering. Some people need to cross a desert to appreciate the rain. Never despair of those you care for - keep your arms open and they will return home.

Rikki Beadle-Blair

What I learned today #141

To bring an end to the self-criticism of the body that houses and clothes my restless soul – it's time to show full appreciation for its grace, power, honesty and resilience - carrying me day after day with purpose through this world, over land, through water and into the air; a cradle for those I care for and a sanctuary for those I love. I will stretch it, explore it, strengthen it and humbly celebrate it.

What I learned today #142

Wherever you are, you got yourself there. Whatever you've got is what you've saved. You are who you are as a result of how you've behaved. Welcome to your choices. Life is a list of consequences and your next move will define who you are in that instant and who you'll become in the next. Luck does not exist, good or bad - there only ever was, and only ever will be you. Who are you going to be?

Rikki Beadle-Blair

What I learned today 143

Our parents are not grown-ups. Not as mature, supportive and unselfish as we would like them to be? Look again: They're children too, let down and wounded by Mummy and Daddy, just like us, still waiting for a reason why - but for so many years longer. What would happen if we gave them what we've been missing? Who would we be if we provided a fund of unconditional love? Are we ready to be grown-ups with the open soul of the accepting child?

What I learned today 144

Everything we long for or admire has no more than the power we give it. The National Theatre, the Royal Court, Broadway, the Olympics, the Oscars are all projections. Prestige, passion, creativity and progress are available right now from the only source that can satisfy you; the source of your yearning ambition, the source of the power of the West End and Hollywood... You. You are Hollywood.

Rikki Beadle-Blair

What I learned today #145

There is no greater feeling than falling into bed at the end of the day, knowing that you have done the right thing with your time; that you have been your authentic self, investing entirely in your true passion without hesitation or distraction; that you have connected with those you have encountered and you have moved forward in unity - that you have truly lived.

What I learned today #146

Your life is defined not by the actions of others, but by the quality of your responses. Respond with grace and openness and that is the life you will be living; welcome challenges with wit and joyful resilience and that is the person you will be; approach all you encounter with empathy and understanding and that is the world you will be living in. A world of connection. A world you have made.

Rikki Beadle-Blair

What I learned today #147

We are so much stronger than even we realise. Within us are untapped reserves of courage, creativity, intelligence and plain old-fashioned strength - all we need to carry us over the roughest seas. If we stay calm, stay authentic and trust our instincts, we can surf tsunamis and stay standing. Own ourselves and we own the world.

What I learned today #148

Inspiration is everywhere, in everyone. Look around at all the faces layered with lives, calling for someone to draw them, photograph them, set them to music, write their biography. So many truths to tell, assumptions to challenge, achievements to celebrate. Express Us, expand Us - tell our stories. Remind us that, even though we may be lonely, we are never alone.

Rikki Beadle-Blair

What I learned today #149

When it gets too dark - light up. When the door slams in your face - open up. When the load gets too heavy - pick yourself up. The wild in you will scare them, the child in you will shame them - don't shame or scare yourself. If the path's too narrow - expand. If the ceiling's too low - break through. Stand up and never lie down until you're all used up – but be yourself and you never will be.

What I learned today #150

It starts with the first thing I eat, the first words I say, the way I open my eyes. When I hug the day to me like a bouquet, inhale its scent. Those days when I truly awaken, celebrate the wonder of my strong body, the phenomenon of my enquiring mind and the valour of my questing soul – those are the days my life erupts with purpose and I take off like the winged horse I was born to be.

Rikki Beadle-Blair

What I learned today #151

There is a choice of worlds available to us. We can wither away marooned on a desert island feeling isolated while waiting to be rescued, or we can explore this fertile paradise and enjoy the adventure. If you live in a world of lack it's a decision - if you live a lonely life, it's by choice - and if you're bored, you're working at it. So many worlds, so many choices, so many lives... All yours.

What I learned today #152

We never lose anyone. Once they've passed through our lives, the faint ghost of them lingers. If they move on and slip out of our orbit, the lesson of them remains. Freedom needs movement and to attempt to restrict another's journey, however adored their company, flies in the face of life - which requires change and so inevitably includes the mysterious richness of death.

Rikki Beadle-Blair

What I learned today #153

Sometimes it's okay to walk away. If you're not bringing out the best in someone, why stick around? We don't need to judge them, we don't have to banish them or make them feel bad for who they are or what they've done. We don't have to fix them - or engage with them at all. Sometimes understanding means realising that your work here is complete. It's Over... Let Go... And Now...

What I learned today #154

Never panic. It never works. When the pressure is on, it's a chance to show who you really are; to draw on your resources. Dig deep, clear your mind, avoid distractions, focus and come alive. This is your moment - seize it and soar.

Rikki Beadle-Blair

What I learned today #155

Paradise is purpose. If you uncover your passion and find a way to share it with the world and give your spirit over to what you love most without fear or hesitation , the sky opens up and there is Heaven above you - the ground falls away and there is Heaven below - the walls dissolve and Eden springs up all around. Existence with direction is life most deeply lived.

What I learned today #156

It's within those big challenges - those crunch-points when it could all just fall apart – that you find out who you really are. Savour adversity. There's no greater trainer.

Rikki Beadle-Blair

What I learned today #157

We always know what to do – we just don't always want to do it. We know what eat, what relationships to avoid, how to get fit and healthy, how to behave and treat others. We know what we need to learn and how to make the best of what we have. If we listen to our best selves, if we can just take our own advice and do the work required, what a life awaits us. What a life.

What I learned today #158

Embody the change that you wish to see in others. If you think it's doable then prove it. If you need understanding, give understanding, if you demand tolerance then tolerate intolerance - deploying your wealth of experience to understand where others are in their journey. If you hope for an enlightened world - light up. Illuminate the way.

Rikki Beadle-Blair

What I learned today #159

Progress needs a plan. Without one, desires and dreams are just vain clutter. Write it all down and read it out loud. Pinpoint what you want to achieve and why you want to achieve it. Be fearless and truthful. Next, announce to yourself that you are going to achieve it. Then ask yourself why you haven't already. What have you not done? That's what you have do. Now do it.

What I learned today #160

Of course I believe in miracles. In the mirror we witness a cluster of impossibilities; every movement - the regular expansion and contraction of our breathing, the joyous explosion of our laughter, the complex catalogue of silent expression in one falling tear – God's gift or cosmic accident, a mind-boggling, impossible fact. A mini-reflection of the Universe. Limitless. Miraculous. Alive.

Rikki Beadle-Blair

What I learned today #161

Look around - everyday gestures, graceful and awk-ward, expressing friendship, love, hope, fear. Fleeting touches, kisses, smiles; shy interactions, liberating surrenders to the creative instinct, wild demonstrations of overwhelming unreasonable feeling. Crack the fragile codes of Us in motion - hear the silent cries for connection - understand your 'enemy' and family and see that they are one.

What I learned today #162

There are the places you're supposed to want to be and the places you belong. No one else is qualified to define what success means to you – it's not their job to assess and value your achievements. Success is not defined by how you are seen, but by how (and who) you see. Not by what you have but by what you can afford to share. Not by where you are, but how happy you are to be here.

Rikki Beadle-Blair

What I learned today #163

There is no time in this busy life for bullshit. No dawdling, no dodging, self-hatred, no self-dismissal, no disappointment, no laziness, no self-destruction, no addiction, no poison, no judgements, no dishonesty, no feuds, no envy, no grievances, no revenge, no blame, no anger, no hunger, no greed, no frustration, no rage, no ego, no lies. Just love - Just truth - Just life.

What I learned today #164

When you're feeling too tired to have your photo taken, too old to flirt, too stressed to feel anything but ugly, remember: happiness is the only true beauty. So smile - light up your face, light up your day, the room, your life, the world. Go further: throw back your head and laugh. And there you are - too busy being happy to be anything else but gorgeous.

Rikki Beadle-Blair

What I learned today #165

Do it now. Clean as you go; address things up front; let nothing fester. Procrastination is the thief of life. Don't put off awkward conversations, speak up and get it said. Get emails answered, admin seen to, make deals with your creditors, get the laundry spinning. Free yourself for the juicy life: working to bring your vision to the world, living, loving, laughing and dancing your ass off.

What I learned today #166

In the end all that matters is Love; the only thing that will heal you, the only hope for peace. Anger won't carry you forward to where you want to live; retribution will leave your stomach growling - bloated and empty. If can you finally love (without condoning) your attacker, your burglar, your abuser, your assassin, you will expand like a smile... as glowing and life-giving as the sun.

Rikki Beadle-Blair

What I learned today #167

This is my world. My sky, my sea - every drop - every grain of salt, every breeze, every beat of every wing. Mine. I don't need a permit to be here, I cannot be denied. I belong. I fit. I have no enemies, only family - no competitors, only peers. In my world, everyone belongs - everyone fits. This is my world - this is my life. And whatever you think of me, you are welcome. You fit.

What I learned today #168

Every inch of you belongs. Every lump and bump, every smile, every scar, is a vital part of everything. Every screw-up a contribution - every triumph an inspiration. Don't think for even one slippery second that we can do without you. This is all is incomplete without you. Withhold nothing of yourself. Sing, dance and act; wrap your arms around us and share your story. We need you.

Rikki Beadle-Blair

What I learned today #169

Rage is a jail. Anger liberates no one. What's required to take effective action is calm intent and the clear-eyed thrill of purpose - And truth. With truth we free the slaves, we uplift the downtrodden and rescue the furious oppressors from their prison. With truth we can save lives and preserve our souls. Truth is the only effective weapon. Truth cannot miss. Truth is freedom.

What I learned today #170

Bitterness is laziness; providing a convenient paralysis that keeps you from being where you said you wanted to be, doing what you claimed you wanted to do, feeling what you swore you wanted to feel. Drop the victim alibi and say a loving thank you to those who have set the bar so high. Without them your leap would not be so high, without them you would not be as strong.

Rikki Beadle-Blair

What I learned today #171

Frustration is a distraction. Energy best employed to take you forward is frittered on false blame and a bogus belief system. Cease dawdling about wishing that the world was made for those with limited imaginations - it wasn't. It was made for you at your brightest, most creative, most passionate and most authentic. Relax, appreciate the challenge and rise to it. No distractions. Just you.

What I learned today #172

Resentment is pointless. Precious time frittered away on something already gone. Whatever was said or done is over. The current era is the only one you have now - why waste it force-feeding your ego over and over with rehashed pain? Stop wishing you had a different history, start mining your experience for education and give thanks for your teachers. However painful the lesson - you're smarter now.

Rikki Beadle-Blair

What I learned today #173

Sorry won't kill you. Sometimes it needs to be heard. Sometimes it needs to be said. If you're waiting to hear it, then one word from you can change that. It's not about who's most wrong. Tend your own garden - can you swear you're entirely innocent? If not, lead by example: Let go of the need to win, put down your pride and speak up. Better to do right than to be right.

What I learned today #174

I've never met a soul who could not be a star. Appearance is no hindrance, background no barrier. All that matters is your work ethic and commitment to who you really are. You are a sex symbol, you are an icon to someone. The encouragement your existence brings to bothers is required. Find the best context to present your true self without fear, and you will shine.

Rikki Beadle-Blair

What I learned today #175

This is your youth. The age you are now will never come again - live it like the child you are, let the wonder of everything overwhelm you, lift you. Never surrender to the ignorance of cynicism, never waste time being jaded, never fool yourself that you've seen or heard it all. Look for the surprise in everything. Stay fresh. Stay as young as you are 'til the day you die.

What I learned today #176

Persistence is key. Once is an event, regularly is a culture – every day is a lifestyle. A trickle of water will carve through a mountain given time. Desire is not enough. To get what you really want, you need to keep wanting it, keep loving it, keep living it. And the love you want, the body you want, the career you want will be yours - and the life you want will be the life you have.

Rikki Beadle-Blair

What I learned today #177

You are your habits. No matter what you call yourself or claim to be, you are not what you do occasionally, but what you do consistently. If you spend every day on the couch, you are a spectator not an athlete. Runners run, dancers run, actors act. To become what you want to be, you must begin. Pick up that pen, fill in that application, find that trainer, open your mouth and sing.

What I learned today #178

Be happy for those who have what you want - the money, the lover, the home, the career - they are proof that it's attainable. Any negativity focused towards your desire will simply repel it. Envy is never attractive - it offers you nothing. Abandon your cultivated poverty and habitual wretchedness, celebrate the fortune around you and become instantly rich, successful, lovable and beautiful.

Rikki Beadle-Blair

What I have learned today #179

The key to success: Commit to the work you love. Eat it, drink it, breathe it, let it become a part of your DNA. Make yourself an expert in your passion, become a pioneer. Forget about what you can earn. Don't concern yourself with the affirmation of others. Become what you love and you become money. Become your passion and you become a star.

What I learned today #180

To mind my own business. It is not my job to make everyone happy, or to insist that they do 'the right thing' or the 'healthy' thing. If I truly believe in freedom I must accept how others choose to exercise it. Each of us has our own path, and we all have the right to be unhappy. I can offer to share my kindness, loyalty, honesty, support, understanding and love. The rest is up to them.

Rikki Beadle-Blair

What I learned today #181

It is not death we need to fear - but life unlived.

What I learned today #182

While asking our family to love and accept us as we are, perhaps it's time to ask ourselves - can we love and accept them as they are, with all their criticisms, contradictions, irritants, failings and flaws? Can we love ourselves as we are? Why wait for others to do what needs to be done? Love is power. Why not be powerful and give the gift we hope to receive.

Rikki Beadle-Blair

What I learned today #183

Somewhere behind everything is love. Every crime, every cruelty, every kiss, every gift, every lie, is an attempt to offer, instigate, evade, recover from or cry out for affection or acknowledgement. Whether our response is to reward or to punish, it will find its true power, justice and value if born out of the cradle of understanding that rocks within all of us: the cradle of love.

What I learned today #184

People will get away with whatever you let them. That's the spirit of the child in everyone. Knowing this we can put aside our ego and make a practical plan without entering into empty power games and escalating the drama. No one can walk over you - because no one is above you. Before retaliating, think, "Is this reaction equal to me or beneath me? Am I hoping to get away with something?"

Rikki Beadle-Blair

What I learned today #185

There are no dregs - just juice. Savour the last drop like it's the first, devour the last crumb and enjoy its flavour. Celebrate the passing of each year, each day, each instant, as what it is - the birth of the next - until the final rebirth embraces you. Every breath is someone somewhere's first or last. Respect it, honour it, celebrate it.

What I learned today #186

The best way forward is to harness your impulses. Acknowledging your true passions is an awakening, pursuing them with single-minded zeal is life-changing. It starts with your focus, a pen, some paper, and the courage it takes to own your ambition and abilities. It starts when you decide. It starts with you.

Rikki Beadle-Blair

What I learned today #187

You make the moment. Whatever situation we are in, it's nothing more than that - a situation. Your interpretation alone labels it good luck or bad luck, cataclysm or benefaction. It's all about perspective - and the offer (remember, there's always an offer) is to cave in, curl up and surrender... or soar. When in doubt - spread your wings. Soar.

What I learned today #188

Only boring people ever get bored. If someone is not holding your attention, you're not asking the right questions – you're not looking at the right things. In a world packed with fascinating people, every interaction is an opportunity to gain knowledge and insight. So much to learn. Education waits in everyone you meet. Look and listen. Enjoy.

Rikki Beadle-Blair

What I learned today #189

Nothing ever dies, it just becomes something else. Every time we wake is rebirth, an invitation to become who really are and deserve to be. Every heartbeat is a chance for us to finally come to life as ourselves and experience each breath as what it is: the first and last of its kind.

What I learned today #190

The validation you seek is within you, the appreciation you hunger for is your own. You are bigger than an award, deeper than a review, more engulfing than any applause. You cannot be outnumbered. Free others from the ridiculous responsibility of assessing your worth; commit to giving out the encouragement you desire and watch your world expand to a universe.

Rikki Beadle-Blair

What I learned today #191

You are the ocean. You are the sky, the clouds, the earth itself. Nothing can overshadow you except you yourself, nothing can distract you or impede you. Nothing can keep you earthbound more than fear and distrust in who you are and always were - a child of creation. Let go of hesitation and commit to the land-scape within you, be the world you are - and offer freedom to all who visit you.

What I have learned today #192

Why aspire when you can inspire? Somewhere there's a small child who's waiting for a role model like you - someone who redefines strength and beauty - who shifts the parameters of what's achievable - who blows apart the myths of what little boys and girls can grow up to be. Stand up and be the dream that others dream. Give hope. Be the icon you are.

Rikki Beadle-Blair

What I learned today #193

Take time to make time. Give yourself headspace to take stock and you can travel so much further, so much faster, so much more joyfully and - most crucially - in the right direction. Sometimes to make that great leap forward we first need to be where we are and advance from there: eat right, plan right, rest right, make those legs strong, get the mind in focus and the rear in gear, crouch down low... then jump.

What I learned today #194

The days when it all falls apart are the best days of all - when you're forced to start from scratch and build something new. You can't hide in complacency any longer - you have to face the fact that you deserve something better. Those who have an easy ride don't enjoy the journey, they sleep through it. Welcome the wake-up call. The call to action. The call to life.

Rikki Beadle-Blair

What I learned today #195

It's what we spend that makes us poor, it's what we eat that makes us fat. Or thin. Or tired. Or weak. Save the energy you dissipate blaming others and cursing fate; fate is a myth and powerlessness a cosy lie. As soon as you own the consequences of your every decision you regain possession of your life. Choose your food, friends and purchases wisely. Let the adventure continue - your way.

What I learned today #196

Stop thinking about how things 'should' be. Stop mourning some withheld circumstance. Rejection of the situation is pointless and deluded. You can't change what you don't acknowledge. Once you abandon your thwarted expectations and capitalize on how things are, you can take practical steps towards to what you think they should be. Truth is the greatest teacher of all.

Rikki Beadle-Blair

What I learned today #197

There's no wealth greater than the privilege of helping others. When your thinking goes from 'What can I get?' to 'What can I give?' your attention shifts towards what you have, and your world-view transforms from a life of lack to a life of luxury. You become the wishing well that others queue to drink from, and throw their coins into; the good fortune they have prayed for. You become a blessing.

What I learned today #198

Happiness is a habit - formed by our deeds, our words, our inner dialogues. An audit of our belief system can bring dividends. Are you a sad Cinderella starving for a banquet while your pumpkin goes mouldy waiting for a fairy godmother? Or are you an entrepreneur capitalizing on the potential for growth in everything you touch? Happiness takes practice - But it pays off.

Rikki Beadle-Blair

What I learned today #199

Creativity is strength. Creativity builds cities, homes, families, communities. When we're silenced, creativity finds our voice, when we're lost, creativity finds our way. Rehabilitating and enlightening, exploring the space between us to find the invisible skin that connects everything. Creativity frees the prisoner and the slave. Creativity will save our children. Creativity is the way.

What I learned today #200

These little explosions of joy that spring out of little hidden places like a playful pet - triggered by a bite of warm buttered toast, an unexpectedly perfect sky or an innocent smile from someone beautiful, unaware of just how deeply adored they are at that moment - these treasures lie waiting inside almost everything and everyone, waiting to be unwrapped and appreciated. Look a little closer.

Rikki Beadle-Blair

What I learned today #201

There is a calm that comes from knowing who you are.
A peace that protects you from fear and paralysing self-
doubt. The realisation that we have nothing to prove,
just a destiny to fulfil that only we have the power to
choose. With self-knowledge we abandon all romanticizing of suffering. Pain becomes a tiny part of life, to
be valued but not coveted. And love, life and joy become one.

What I learned today #202

I've been so unambitious - wanting the success of
others - their talent, beauty, love-lives. But that's all
been done. This beauty and talent may not be standard;
it might never be popular, but it's brand new – it's
pioneering - and it's mine. Nothing is more ambitious
in this world than having the confidence to be yourself.
That's what true talent and beauty is. The Art of being
You.

Rikki Beadle-Blair

What I learned today #203

Nothing you need is out of your reach. Nothing you truly want. Nothing that matters. You were born with every luxury and every capability – they are all are just parts of you that you forgot about while 'growing up'. Reach inward... there it is inside you, where it's always been. Nourish it, help it grow, expand with it. Become the universe you are, filled with countless worlds, all bearing your name.

What I learned today #204

Do we really see those we love or reduce them to a word? Lover, Brother, Sister, Friend, Boss Mum, Dad - are these people or positions? When we name each other do we lose sight of who we are? What if we take away the function and see the person there - more than social furniture, more than what we're in the habit of needing them to be? Who are they when we see beyond the title? Who are we?

Rikki Beadle-Blair

What I learned today #205

Who we really are is what's left when you take away the clothes, money, transport and technology, fear of darkness and terror of dying. The part of us that can stand naked without a mirror to reassure or punish us and just be there without needing assessment. The voice within that says, 'I am no more or less than everything and that's enough.' That's who we are. Something simply lovely. ...This.

What I learned today #206

Future happiness is an illusion. Past happiness is a trap. The only real happiness is this truth right here that's immediately available. You can suffer until lunchtime or you can enjoy the feeling of lightness. You can trudge across the desert, eyes fixed on the mirage that never gets closer - or enjoy your adventure in the sun. Be where you are - you can't ever be anywhere else.

Rikki Beadle-Blair

What I learned today #207

This moment is the foundation for every future moment - how are you investing in it? If, instead of waiting on some external trigger for pleasure, we choose to cultivate the habit of finding the thrill that lies right now right here, then we can take control of our mood and sustain joy for life. Disappointment is a choice, dissatisfaction is a habit, and so is happiness. What do you choose?

What I learned today #208

Instead of hoping for more cash and possessions or 'better' circumstances, I need to work towards the grace needed to cope with not getting what I thought I wanted and the presence required to deal with worse situations. I'm ready to welcome the perspective that comes with life's challenges. Being privileged is never as enriching as being resilient - and nowhere near as useful. Bring it on.

Rikki Beadle-Blair

What I learned today #209

Life owes you nothing more than it's already given you
- the breath that's in your body. Whatever you want the
world to bring you, you can bring to the world. You can
make all those you meet feel like Oscar winners, sex
symbols, geniuses and great company. Who holds the
magic, the star or the star-maker? The whole world is
waiting for someone to ask them to dance. Make the
first move and change your world.

What I learned today #210

I have nothing to hide - wrinkles, love handles, mess
and mistakes - they are all mine, the map of my life so
far. We can make improvements and adjustments, but
we don't have to pretend to have been born flawless
and we don't need to live in shame. This is my age. This
is my face. These are my scars. This is my history. Now
watch the amazing places it takes me.

Rikki Beadle-Blair

What I learned today #211

Forget about 'Then'. Then is either done with or hasn't happened yet. All the healing you need is already here. All the pain you've suffered was worth it. Feel the breath and warmth in your body - claim the life rushing through you. This particular golden era will never come again - celebrate it. Enjoy your amazing self, savour this thrilling journey, treasure this immaculate step.

What I learned today #212

It begins with the truth. Those sublime bursts of cool water relief that come with clear-eyed honesty, when you can see every element of discontent as the direct result of your decisions past and present and are ready to make new choices. What you eat, what you say, how you treat others, how you allow others to treat you, the pain you harbour and the limits you break. It begins with you.

Rikki Beadle-Blair

What I learned today #213

Even more painful than the passing of loved ones is allowing part of us to die with them, killing them again and again, when in truth they still live - in us, through us. Let's feel the sadness, pay tribute to their value, then celebrate their legacy - treasuring all that their moving on can teach us. Why lose them, or use them to suffer, when we can thank them for teaching us to live?

What I learned today #214

Resistance is useless. The energy you give to what opposes you strengthens it, increasing its power in your life. War weakens you. Hate diverts you. Conflict depletes resources. Love your 'enemy' - appreciate the energy they're expending - observe it, absorb it, make it yours - and grow ever stronger as the opposition burns itself out, unwittingly donating all its power to you.

Rikki Beadle-Blair

What I learned today #215

Being broke is a blessing: Our chance to be creative with how we find entertainment; our opportunity to capitalize on what we already have. Time to shop at home - rediscover the wardrobe, raid the bookshelf and the dvd collection and catch up on the unread, the unwatched and the classic inspirations - take time to recharge and relaunch. Building a future is free.

What I learned today #216

Those we love are like moons and stars, shifting and drifting in out of view but still out there somewhere, beyond the clouds, below the horizons - waxing and waning - revolving, evolving. The gravity of friendships can pull us apart. But if we trust the seasons, eventually they bring those we love back into our orbit - together again, ready to share what our journeys have taught us.

Rikki Beadle-Blair

What I learned today #217

Let's get better at being less talented, less brilliant, less complete - unburdened with frozen knowledge. Let us be a little bit lost and just a little bit dumb, wide open and thirsty to drink this life in and hungry to learn - gazing at everything with the fearless genius of a child 'til we fill ourselves to overflowing, and one day perhaps make something brand new and beautiful.

What I learned today #218

It is not when we are loved that we become beautiful - but when we love. Love for those we know preserves us - love for strangers and enemies transforms us. Love without fear, without expectation, without need. Love is one of the world's most coveted treasures - and when we tap into our well of tenderness, we feel wealthy and beautiful - because we are.

Rikki Beadle-Blair

What I learned today #219

Look out of the window - see the sky, catch your reflection and witness the simple perfection of both; hold your hand to your lips, feel the warmth of your breathing, bite an apple and taste the sweetness of the sun, put your head against someone to hear their heartbeat, hold them in your arms and smell their scalp... like it's your first day on Earth. Come to your senses, come back to life.

What I learned today #220

Life takes practise. It is built from our habits - actions repeated until they become our instincts - and eventually our destiny. Choose a new life-story: practise truth, practise fitness, practise creativity, practise courage, practise risk, practise recovery, practise acceptance, practise understanding, practise love - living it, giving it, accepting it, sharing it. Practise life.

Rikki Beadle-Blair

What I learned today #221

You never feel more alive than when pursuing your passions without reservation or hesitation. Knowing you're where you should be, doing what you know you should do is the very definition of the word 'living'. Working with people you respect on projects you believe in defines the word 'fulfilled'. Let nothing divert you from your life's calling. Live your life on purpose.

What I learned today #222

It's not about self-discipline, it's about liberation. It's not about self-deprivation, it's about nourishment. It's not about work work work, it's about inhabiting your days doing what you love. It's not about 'soulmates', it's recognising someone impressive who makes you laugh and learn. It's not about mistakes, it's about seized opportunities. It's not about how you look. It's about how you live.

Rikki Beadle-Blair

What I learned today #223

Everything has its rhythm. Careers, friendships, romances, journeys, projects. You can pick up the tempo and you can slow it down - but once the beat is laid down, the way forward is to respect it. Of course the trick is to be the one who sets it in the first place. Compose your life. Be the conductor not the orchestra. Be the drummer not the dancer.

What I learned today #224

How about instead of stressing about outside wealth, outside growth, outside beauty and outside validation, we turn our efforts and attention to nurturing our inside treasures, expansion, beauty and appreciation? Why not try staging the revolutionary coup of simply loving ourselves? Why envy the garden when you haven't even bloomed yet? Dig deep - you're even more lovely than you look.

Rikki Beadle-Blair

What I learned today #225

In these glittering cities of technology we inhabit, all the toys we have to play with are there to be enjoyed and employed in the pursuit of happiness and progress. But nothing has been invented that can make us think, learn or laugh out loud like the company of those we love. Nothing we can buy can validate us, nothing we can eat can sustain us like affection. Treasure it. Share it.

What I learned today #226

Sexual orientation is an invention. The categories of Gay, Straight and Bi are so much smaller than the epic waves of love, lust and longing that can so entirely overwhelm and sweep us in many more directions than three. It's irrelevant where our impulses take us, so long as we treat one another with kindness and sensitivity. Tenderness is limitless and defies definition. Connection is all.

Rikki Beadle-Blair

What I learned today #227

There are few things more effective than a combination of acceptance and action. Acceptance is essential: First deal with the situation as it is, without being pointlessly sidetracked by wishing things were different. Action is crucial: It's no good making vision-boards out of pretty wishes unless we're prepared to roll up our sleeves to become vision-builders. Acceptance. Action. Results.

What I learned today #228

When we are confronted by gracelessness is when we need to be our most graceful. When we are met by rage is when we are required be gracious. When we witness cruelty, our way forward is kindness. When we encounter hate our saviour is love. Meet your own standards - lead by example. If you want a better world - be better.

Rikki Beadle-Blair

What I learned today #229

Grudges keep you mired in a past that no longer exists. Is the perpetrator of the crime the same person today? Are you? How much of your life do you want to spend as a victim? Understanding evil can transform both it and you beyond recognition. Who knows, perhaps it was never really evil in the first place and you were never a victim. Take control of your response and walk free.

What I learned today #230

Give up struggling and commit to the flow. A commitment to happiness doesn't need to be a battle. Unclench and let go of all nonsense and confusion and listen to the heart that beats beneath all the self-doubt you've been taught. Trust yourself to know what you really need and what's good for you. Be who you really are. Let it be easy.

Rikki Beadle-Blair

What I learned today #231

Opposition is only a problem when it comes from within. Everything else is a challenge to raise your standards. Any chance to strengthen your resolve should be welcomed with open arms. Don't feed your detractors at the expense of your own resources; take any energy directed at you, good or bad - and convert it into fuel to power your mission.

What I learned today #232

This moment has so much to teach you. Instead of taking events at face value - good or bad - we are free to dig in and see what lessons await. The way you deal with any situation decides who you are right now; who you will become is being constructed from your habitual responses - including this one. So... student or dissident, activist or artist - who are you going to be?

Rikki Beadle-Blair

What I learned today #233

I've been so unromantic. Lazy, unimaginative notions of love stolen from movies have led me to endure cruelties, make selfish demands and fetishize disappointment in the pursuit of clichés. My real passion is for the beautiful truth of life. There is a kiss in everything. I claim it. And I share my romance with those I love as they are and not as I dreamed they'd be.

What I learned today #234

Love drives our every action - the search for love, the hope, the dream, the loss of love. The pain of it, the giddy joy of it, the consuming need for it. It's behind everything. But we don't have to ache for it - we don't need to suffer in love's name. If we simply love - truly love, without demand or projection - then every moral question is solved. Love is always the answer.

Rikki Beadle-Blair

What I learned today #235

Surrender to your innocence. You don't always have to strike the worldly pose, you don't need to seem all-knowing and cool. Let that part of you that is wide-eyed keep discovering the world, seeing and feeling everything for the first time. Share your freshness with the world. Let yourself be brand new and take those first bold baby steps towards life.

What I learned today #236

There are days when you recognise that it's time to raise your standards - when you know you're ready to look better, feel better, live better, love better. When you realise it's time to return to the lovely business of fulfilling the destiny that you have determined for yourself. When it's time to take the plan to another level. Amazing days like today.

Rikki Beadle-Blair

What I learned today #237

Being open doesn't have to mean being vulnerable. There's being open and vibrant - being open and free. Being alive to everyone you meet, every opportunity that presents itself, great or small. There's being open to every surprising facet of who you are and the kaleidoscopic opportunities that daring to be yourself can bring you. Being open can spur others to courage. Inspire us. Open up.

What I learned today #238

It won't kill you to be wrong once in a while. Who wants to be right all the time? A rich and rewarding life requires venturing into the darkness away from the campfire to grope and stumble through mysteries. It's a foolish spirit that's unwilling to credit the knowledge of others; it's an ungrateful soul that refuses to benefit from their wisdom. Keep learning - keep growing - keep going.

Rikki Beadle-Blair

What I learned today #239

Defiance for its own sake is an empty exercise - another distraction that delays the journey towards your intended destination. Are you diverting valuable energy towards those who do not get you when you could be saving your efforts to share with others who need and want your full attention and abilities? Passion combined with purpose equals effectiveness. Success makes its own statement.

What I learned today #240

Everyone needs a plan. Especially artists. Instinct is essential, but it's not enough. Passion is crucial - stamina is key – not enough. Decide where you want to go and what you want to achieve there, then devise a strategy. Every great project needs a plot. This is your story - don't be an extra, don't be a walk-on, don't be an actor for hire. Be your own producer and take the lead.

Rikki Beadle-Blair

What I learned today #241

Just because someone has a job, doesn't mean they're good at it - people will let you down. But this is your plan, not theirs. Don't allow your need to be liked to lower your standards, but don't let your impatience derail you from your mission either. Finding diplomatic ways to maintain control of your business while taking responsibility for the quality of your working relationships will define your career. Do your job.

What I learned today #242

It doesn't matter how blessed you were at birth with looks or talent or connections - you still have to do the work. Finding a calling; building a career; maintaining enthusiasm; freedom, friendships, relationships, family, social skills, sex – liking yourself – even having fun... It's all work. And if you do what you love and love what you do – all worth it.

Rikki Beadle-Blair

What I learned today #243

Balance is all. Between endeavour and ease, pride and humility, independence and connection, tenderness and strength, there lies a way to be both focused and open, assertively understanding, sensually pure, beautifully plain, with a disciplined spontaneity and a playful work ethic. A way to be entirely you - nothing crushed, nothing suppressed, everything valued. Balanced.

What I learned today #244

Stop hoping, start providing. Ever noticed when you cook for others that by the time you sit at the table, you're already too full to eat? There is freedom in giving - fulfilment in sharing. Don't wait for the world to give you what you need - everything you need you already have. Start offering what you long for to the world and you will receive it - because you are the world.

Rikki Beadle-Blair

What I learned today #245

Momentum is magic: Gaining it - maintaining it.
Whether it's work or romance (they should be the same
thing anyway), running a race, learning a skill, creating
a project, or pursuing change, it's about putting a work
ethic into action, building connections, developing a
profile, getting into a organic rhythm that propels you
towards your goal. Choose a target. Get up to speed.
Keep going.

What I learned today #246

Progress is not about changing what you are, it's about
revealing who are - having the courage to identify what
you want out of life and finding confidence in what you
have to offer in exchange. Declining to be paralysed by
the possibility of being misunderstood and allowing
yourself to be seen and heard. Making a generous
commitment to perfecting the art of simply being you.

Rikki Beadle-Blair

What I learned today #247

Be grateful for your life exactly as it is. Guess what? You're this tall, you're this rich, you've got this family, you are on this trip. Some of these things can be changed, some of them cannot – all of them can be appreciated. Today is not defined by what it could have been, but by what it is; and so are you. You can wish for better or work for better. The decision is yours.

What I learned today #248

It's all too easy to see where others are going wrong - but is that because you see yourself reflected in them? Are you focusing on the shortcomings of others in order to avoid dealing with your own demons? Remember, trying to control others is a way of avoiding controlling ourselves. The time has come to stop procrastinating. Are you ready to take your own advice?

Rikki Beadle-Blair

What I learned today #249

A special life travels a special path. If you want a
unique career you're gonna need to make some extra
trips to the well. To find a special mentor, special lover
and a special level of resilience, you'll need to travel
uncharted waters and face down demons - including
your own. Standard journeys are for sofa-surfers.
Special takes sweat.

What I learned today #250

To be at ease wherever we are - as comfortable out in
the world as we are in our homes. To journey with
fearless curiosity. Luxuriating in our bodies without
self-consciousness or shame. Wearing our spirits as
skins to soak up the sunlight that bursts out of everything. To be here and go there and share each second of
this reckless whirlwind romance. This is adventure.
This is living.

Rikki Beadle-Blair

What I learned today #251

It's true that travel broadens the mind, but the fastest way to see the world is to see it afresh. No ticket needed, no visa to apply for; just take a fresh look at everything you've taken for granted all these years with the eyes of an infant explorer, hungry to discover and there it is: a whole other world, right where you are - where it's always been - waiting for you to come around.

What I learned today #252

The one prize truly worth having cannot be won, only claimed - this moment, this second, this breath, this heartbeat, fully inhabited. The key, as always, is to become the thing we crave: become happiness, become fulfilment, become a source of wealth; and as soon we surrender to habitually making the present moment magical and sharing it without discrimination - we become the prize.

Rikki Beadle-Blair

What I learned today #253

Betrayal inflicts some of the deepest wounds, even though it doesn't even really exist – only the expectations we harbour for a return on our investments. Clinging to our desires is what creates and maintains suffering. Everyone is doing what they feel is right for them, living in the best way they feel they can - just as you do - and honouring their choices frees us.

What I learned today #254

Listen to yourself. How do you describe yourself on meeting new people? Regularly dismissing yourself with cheery self-deprecation? Is there a running commentary of self-criticism? Constantly calling yourself names? Would you let someone talk to your child, the way you talk to you? If you feel you are surrounded by people who hold you back and put you down - make sure you are not one of them.

Rikki Beadle-Blair

What I learned today #255

Listen. You don't always need to have the last word. Or even any words at all. What sounds like anger could be fear - what sounds like bitterness could be love - a demand might actually be a plea. If you could hush your ego, what would you hear? You might hear the cry from a wound you've inflicted - or a final danger warning that saves you. Listen. You might hear the truth.

What I learned today #256

Kindness is everywhere. We focus so much on things we don't get; gambits we don't win; unanswered requests and slamming doors. But look through your life - how many opportunities came through friends? How many favourite things were gifts? Check your inbox and look at those smiling messages. Drink it all in. Smile back. Give back. Give thanks.

Rikki Beadle-Blair

What I've learned today #257

When in doubt, open your arms - wrap them round someone. Hold them. Rock them. Let them know they're not alone. Reach up to the high and the mighty. No-one thinks to hug the tall people. The bigger they are, the more they need it - the scarier they are, the lonelier they are. No one's too evil to love, no one is so lost that they can never come home. Open your arms - welcome someone home.

What I've learned today #258

To go to the next level requires leaving the level you're on. It's not a betrayal of the hallway to go into the living room. It's not a criticism of the garden to step into your home. Movement is life, Life is change. Progress takes courage, commitment, vision and the occasional heart-stopping dive into the dark. If your spirit is calling you into the storm, don't stay in the cosy warm. Step out.

Rikki Beadle-Blair

What I learned today #259

Find a regular way to work with kids. Let them teach you - encourage them to challenge you - recognise yourself - reconnect with your essence. Nothing is more thrilling, more humbling, more painful or more healing than the headlong collision with truth that occurs in the company of youth. Celebrate who you've been - share who you secretly still are. Stay sharp, stay fresh, stay young.

What I learned today #260

We are all romantics. Inside even the most cynical lies some bruised or fearful idealist, quaking in the shadow of our monumental interdependence - romanticizing the persona of the self-sufficient samurai who will not touched, cannot be claimed, will never be possessed... all the while longing to be tamed; to be special to someone; to love and be loved in return.

Rikki Beadle-Blair

What I learned today #261

This is my time - I define this experience and I can choose the life I want - and I choose not to be angry, frustrated, indecisive or lost. I choose success - I choose happiness; I choose to be fearless, I choose to be healthy and strong; to be alert and understanding. I choose to remain bold, bright and independent. I choose to share. I choose to survive. I choose to live. Because I can.

What I learned today #262

As a kid I secretly believed that I was destined to be a superhero. But a voice in my head would say, 'who do you think you are?' and stop me taking off. Now I know that realising our potential is not arrogance - withholding our contribution is a robbery. I am a superhero, as we are all are - capable of using my powers for the forces of good. Capable of saving the world. And I am ready to fly.

Rikki Beadle-Blair

What I learned today #263

I don't know where the fear comes from that makes us so self-destructive - and don't have the time or need to assign blame. I do know this: Eating well, living well, loving well and being well is a decision. Being early and prepared are decisions; integrity is another. And I am willing to make those resolutions every day and benefit from my choices. Because I want a life that I have chosen.

What I learned today #264

Advice is valuable, but no-one else can determine your worth or destiny. Why set your ambitions by the limitations of other people's vision of you or experience of the world, when you are here to redefine what's beautiful and what's possible? We can be inspired by what's been achieved without repeating it. Unleash your maverick original self without fear or hesitation. Bring about change. Be you.

Rikki Beadle-Blair

What I learned today #265

If instead of examining our opponent's shortcomings we concentrated on their intentions - what they're trying to gain, replace or repair - what might we discover? Empathy can solve perplexing mysteries, understanding can transform our experience and guide us to effective action. Enquire and acquire. Love and learn.

What I learned today #266

Whenever you lie to someone you give away your power. Now, on top of whatever initial fear made you run from the facts, you've added fear of exposure and potential humiliation. And under all that, it's still there - the truth you're attempting to dodge and deny - unchanged - waiting to be dealt with. The truth is a friend. Why make it an enemy?

Rikki Beadle-Blair

What I learned today #267

Sometimes the right move is to stay where you are - be who you've always been and always essentially will be. Others may move away and move on; mistake friendship for a race, climbing over you to get ahead, dropping you for fear your authenticity will feel like a judgement. Hunger makes people desperate. But hold your ground and the wise will return - ready to accept a steady brand of love.

What I learned today #268

If want to change your life - change your mind. It all starts with the way you think - about the world you live in, the people around you and, most crucially, about yourself. When your thinking is balanced and clear, your decisions will be too. When your target is certain, your actions can follow suit. You can achieve anything - IF you really want it and you know why. So ask yourself ...what do you want?

Rikki Beadle-Blair

What I learned today #269

The first time someone attacks you, you're a victim. After that you're an accomplice - a volunteer. When someone is cruel or violent they're telling you who they really are - pay them the respect of believing them the first time. It doesn't help someone who's out of control to indulge or ignore them. The longer you take it, the more confused and enraged they'll be when you stop. Stop now.

What I learned today #270

No one owns me. Every decision is mine. Every bill, every relationship, every word I utter, every choice I make. No one can make me do anything I don't want to and - despite what I may have told myself – no-one ever has. I don't have to conform or rebel. I can write my own story. I can't control what others do, but I can choose how I respond. And I choose to turn my every reaction into art.

Rikki Beadle-Blair

What I learned today #271

Anger is defeat. If I'm to be effective in this world there is no room for wounded, howling ego, impotent explosions, sulking self-pity and the deluded need for others to satisfy my needs. When I raise my voice, it's a child talking. When I feel the hot rush of rage, my focus blurs. When I am calm and clear-headed my aim is true. I have work to do - and I want to enjoy every second of it.

What I learned today #272

We don't have to own everything. We can admire something without coveting it. One can appreciate something without possessing it. What a liberation to give up needing; to be as happy to leave the rose in the sun as to wear it. To window-shop without craving; to find satisfaction in what things are and not what they will make us; to become rich by living within our means.

Rikki Beadle-Blair

What I learned today #273

There are places for each of us where our spirits can sleep or stretch or run naked without hesitation or question. Places where we flow. Some kind of stage, studio, study, store, field, farm, forest, office - or in someone's arms. However it appears to others, for us it's a sacred place - and when we discover it, we find the God in us and miracles occur. Miracles that we have made.

What I learned today #274

It's easy to adore the beautiful, the kind, the accommodating. But why should the immediately lovable have the lion's share of love? Let's save some affection for the disaffected; let's administer a dose of love to the unlovable. Who knows? It might be just what's needed. Sometimes love takes strength.

Rikki Beadle-Blair

What I learned today #275

People are not stepping-stones. We can learn from others, gain from them, make progress through our acquaintance; but if we can contribute our grateful respect - regardless of any initial return – that's the world we'll be helping create, and the benefits will be multiplied for all; not only long-term but in that character-defining instant. In a selfish society, integrity is its own reward.

What I learned today #276

It is no one else's duty to validate us - or even notice us. The only rejection that matters is when we reject ourselves. As long as we keep the faith - celebrating our achievements, expanding our capabilities and promoting our potential - our investment will be sound and our returns will abound. Self-belief and humility are our perfect partners - for work, love and life.

Rikki Beadle-Blair

What I learned today #277

When you find yourself feeling disheartened, disenchanted, disillusioned - forget about yourself and go and help somebody. Donate your time, your expertise, your listening ear, your loving arms. Help someone feel the way you would like to feel - significant, supported, special. Because they are.

What I learned today #278

To have faith in people, regardless of whether they have faith in me; to see the potential in everyone, whether or not they see it in themselves. It's not my business to demand or indulge, but to share my belief and offer my assistance is a worthy passion. There is no greater gift to the world than faith. Wisely employed, faith can change lives.

Rikki Beadle-Blair

What I learned today #279

What you say matters: the words you hear every day inspire or limit you. What you do matters: your life is crafted from consequences. What you value matters: that guides your desires. How you think matters: that's what defines what you'll dare to try. And what you believe matters most of all - because that decides what you achieve.

What I learned today #280

There is nothing more exhausting than doing nothing. A refuelling rest is essential, but oversleeping can leave you weak. Indecision delays progress. Surrendering to helplessness is a debilitating disease. Everyone is agreed on one thing: This world could do with improvement. And improvement - like charity - starts at home – with each of us taking action to make this life all it can be.

Rikki Beadle-Blair

What I learned today #281

Sometimes the smartest thing you can do is allow yourself to be stupid; stop trying to clever and let yourself be taught; be an empty vessel and get filled by the well; take your hands off the wheel to let someone else drive and embark on new adventures. Abandon wisdom for spell and let your naive child ask why and why not. Where's the fun in having nothing left to learn?

What I learned today #282

In the face of our family we see what we've run away from and have never escaped. We see where we've come from and what we could become. There lies the root of all our choices in love and the spark for our philosophies. Why spend time in conflict trying to challenge or change our relations? It's quicker just to love them and let them remind us who we really are. It's better just to live.

Rikki Beadle-Blair

What I learned today 283

If you really know who are then the journey becomes clear. If you can honour your essence at all times you will always know what to say, what decision to make, what road to take. You'll know what you can withstand and absorb, you'll know when to gracefully draw the line. Know yourself and you are never alone, never afraid, never defeated, never lost. Know yourself and you are always home.

What I learned to #284

Find what you love and surrender to it, know what you would die for and live for that. Don't be found guilty of giving too little, withholding your genius because you are afraid it's not desirable. Wanted or not, you are needed. Give yourself, freely, generously, passionately - share your wildest most reckless unrealistic self and welcome yourself to the world.

Rikki Beadle-Blair

What I learned today #285

Is it really too late to follow your heart and go the way your blood beats? Surely it's too late not to. Life is wonderful but short; let go of modesty and all other forms of limited thinking. Be arrogant enough to admit you know what you want. Be brave enough to defy convention; be creative enough to write your own script and cast yourself as the star. Live as a visionary. It's about time.

What I learned today #286

If you had someone else's life, it wouldn't be easier, it would just be a different kind of hard. You have only been offered challenges you can meet, you have only been given problems you handle. If you want an easier ride, give yourself one: Stop expending energy on mourning how fortunate you could be, start capitalizing on how blessed you are and see what kind of life you have then.

Rikki Beadle-Blair

What I learned today #287

It's in those rock-bottom periods that I've been forced to review my situation and make those crucial changes. When my mind has been at its clearest and most decisive. Time to punch through the clouds and pull down the stars to build something new. Now I welcome the days when it all falls apart - here comes the breakthrough, here comes the big bang, here come the stars.

What I learned today #288

When you don't know which way to go - go towards integrity. When you don't know what to say - say something true. When you don't know what to do - do something real. When you're not certain of who to be - be kind. When you're unsure how to be strong - be brave. When you're not sure of what to choose - choose love. True, real, kind & brave - love is integrity. Love is never wrong.

Rikki Beadle-Blair

What I learned today #289

Being lonely is a waste. Savour each precious moment you have to yourself, every golden opportunity to be unapologetically, unselfconsciously you. Seize the chance to listen to yourself, take stock and make plans. Date yourself, celebrate yourself, buy yourself flowers, give yourself the undivided attention you need and deserve. If you can't enjoy your own company, why should anyone else?

What I learned today #290

Early is on time. Arrive calmly, prepared and rested, time to say hello, ready to go. Tardiness is absence. Running behind is running backwards. Lateness is a failure to show up, a hesitation. It's your body-language shouting that you're unwilling or unready. To the pioneer, on time is late. Be there waiting for your peers with big, wide welcoming arms. Lead the way. Arrive.

Rikki Beadle-Blair

What I learned today #291

There's no point to life if you forget to have fun. If you can't laugh about it, you're missing the point of it. When you devote each day to finding ways to enjoy everything, you uncover our true vocation - the pursuit of happiness - and the day fills with victories. If you can jump on every storm that hits you and surf it, what a life you will have, what an inspiration you will be.

What I learned today #292

Get up early if you want to get things done. Get up earlier if you want to get better. Breakfast like a champion and utilise the springboard hours. Plan for quality. Prepare for the unexpected. Gather pet projects and give them the 100% that matches the level of your desire. Enhance the quality of your vision with the depth of your commitment. Stretch yourself. Surpass yourself.

Rikki Beadle-Blair

What I learned today #293

When you don't know what to do, it's time to do
something new. You can't guarantee that others will get
it, but you can choose to do what keeps your heart
pumping. Sharpen the saw, keep the flame under your
feet, stay reckless, stay truthful, stay fresh. Make a sage
youthful contribution. Invent. Adapt. Create.

What I learned today #294

No one knows how young they are. In ten years, the age
you are today will be the age you wish could be again.
Be it now. Leap up in the mornings and seize the day
like someone with their whole life ahead of them.
Dance around in your naked skin and make children
jealous of your energy, courage and boundless enthusiasm. Make the most of your age and your youth. Live it
down. Live it up.

Rikki Beadle-Blair

What I learned today #295

If you want to take your hands off the wheel, make sure you keep your eyes on the road. If you work with an agent, a manager, a producer, accountant, nanny, cleaner or any other intermediary, assistant or representative, don't make them responsible for your security or satisfaction. You are the CEO of your company. The buck stops with you. Enjoy your ride - stay awake.

What I learned today #296

Having a purpose is the key to creative survival. When cash doesn't flow, when doors slam, projects tank and it's back to scratch, you need to refuel with passion. If you know what you're working for, you can tap reserves you never realised you had. If it has real value to you, you can dedicate your life to it. If it doesn't, find what does and do that.

Rikki Beadle-Blair

What I learned today #297

When you feel powerless in this world, get out and find a great view, take a drink of cool water there, take a deep breath, and know for sure that this is your world and that regardless of what you earn or what you own you are enough. Then go about the business of sharing that fact with everyone you meet. And when you veer off course, go back to that simple apex of truth: 'I am enough.'

What I learned today #298

If we want to be loved, appreciated and celebrated, we need to lead the way by example. If we treat ourselves with the respect and affection everyone deserves, we can demonstrate not only how lovable we are, but how deeply we can love. And what could be more beautiful than that?

Rikki Beadle-Blair

What I learned today #299

There's another way of looking at it all. Instead of 'What do I want?' there's 'What have I got?' Instead of 'What have I lost?' – 'What can I share?' Rather than 'What has been stolen?' – 'What can I give?' Such a welcome relief to take time off from longing to concentratie on our wealth. It's not what we accumulate that makes us rich, but what we can afford to give away.

What I learned today #300

No one who ever achieved anything ever told others that it couldn't be done. Don't take your advice from the fearful or the defeated - turn to trailblazers for your inspiration and instruction. Courage is contagious. Catch some.

Rikki Beadle-Blair

What I learned today #301

When we say 'I don't have time' we're really saying 'I don't want to.' Be honest with yourself about what really matters to you. As long as you have the luxury of living, you have time to pursue your true ambitions. Take the time to identify what you need to learn, long to experience, were born to contribute. Decide what must be done and get started. Find time, make time. This is your time.

What I learned today#302

Let's wait 'til there actually is a problem before we have it. Let's not mourn Summer before Autumn arrives. Why not just enjoy the sun? It's one thing to be sensible and figure out what might happen so we can make plans – it's another to strain your neck looking up for circling vultures. If there's to be drama it'll come soon enough. What's the hurry?

Rikki Beadle-Blair

What I learned today #303

To release the past. To love my ex-lovers without expecting them to love me, forgive me, repay, repair, or even remember me. To rejoice in the memory of absent friends without grieving or grudge. To remember all my rejections without resentment, recall each triumph without pining to revisit the high. To free ourselves from our history while acknowledging its legacy. To let be and just be.

What I learned today #304

It's not arrogant to aspire to the greats. Observe the best - absorb their essence, pay tribute to their triumphs. It's an insult to do anything less. Whoever wows you, be it Prophet, Artist, Actor, Rockstar or Revolutionary, you owe it to them to carry their legacy, take it all to the next level and be the upcoming legend. Select an inspiration, make them into a foundation - and build.

Rikki Beadle-Blair

What I learned today #305

Luck is a skill. It needs development like every other talent. We have to embrace the good fortune we have - nurture and expand on it until we master it. We need to become experts on luck, champions in the sport of providence. Learning to tame our blessings, saddle them and ride them home – that's the trick. That's the knack. We have to be our own godsends.

What I learned today #306

Stop chasing your dreams - get strong enough and fast enough that your dreams chase you.

Rikki Beadle-Blair

What I learned today #307

To look for beauty. Wherever I am, whoever I'm talking to. No matter what their status or stature, no matter what they've said or done or what crimes they've committed, there is beauty somewhere there - as there is everywhere - sometimes obvious, often obscure. If we let that discovery inspire us, and behave with intent to pay tribute - whatever course of action we take will be beautiful.

What I learned today #308

For a healthy body - Clean teeth 3 times a day. Find way to sweat 5 times a week. Get 20 minutes of sun a day. Wear sun-block. Walk a lot. Get a health check once a year. Laugh at least once an hour. Avoid drugs. Avoid drunks. Two pints a day or less. 8 glasses of water a day or more. Less sugar. Less caffeine. Less flour. Less fried. Take the stairs. Take vitamins. Eat vegetables. Stretch.

Rikki Beadle-Blair

What I learned today #309

For a healthy mind - Talk to yourself. Encourage yourself. Seek supportive peers. Maintain friendships. Always get dressed, even if you're not going out. Focus on your inner peace not your noisy neighbours. Budget wisely. Keep your home bright, comfortable and clean. Ask for help. Eat well. Sleep well. Exercise. Sing. Dance. Socialise. Communicate. Cry. Laugh. Relax.

What I learned today #310

For a healthy love-life: don't try to change anything that was there when you met your partner. If they hit you, do everyone a favour and say goodbye the first time. Don't humiliate them in company. Always kiss hello & goodbye. Say I love you every day. Tell everyone how beautiful they are. Don't withhold sex. Sulking is rarely sexy. Never expect lovers to be mind-readers. Speak up. Listen. Don't lie. Be kind.

Rikki Beadle-Blair

What I learned today # 311

Sleep is a need, but it's not a right. It has to be earned.
If our days are unsatisfying, our nights will be too. On
the other hand, if you need an alarm to wake you up
you're either not getting enough sleep or you need
something to get up for. Don't feed the stress by lying
awake trying to worry yourself to sleep. Spend the time
planning fulfilling days. Go to bed satisfied.

What I learned today #312

We are not our jewellery, our phones or toys. We're not
our money. We are not even our homes. What we are
cannot be stolen or even borrowed – it can only ever be
shared. Remember, it is far more disheartening to have
to steal than to be stolen from. Whatever thieves sneak
in, we remain undiminished. We are gifts to the world.
We get what we give.

Rikki Beadle-Blair

What I learned today #313

You are what you think. Your thoughts become your life. A bitter spirit cannot contribute to a sweet world. Rage will never bring peace, frustration will not give birth to satisfaction. Focus on the beauty and brilliance that surrounds you and that is what you will see. Think like a lover, a champion, a fulfilled free spirit who is blessed to be here – and that is what you will be.

What I learned today #314

Some people will welcome you – and some will build moats, put up fences, draw lines on the earth and invent borders. But this is your world, every speck of it. And you belong in it. When you look in the mirror, don't do what they taught you – don't cut yourself up and wish parts of you away. Dark or light, large or small, standard or unique, you are all yours. And you belong in you.

Rikki Beadle-Blair

What I learned today #315

Wherever we go in the world, whoever we talk with, we encounter the same basic concerns and needs. The need for sustenance, the need for warmth – and, most of all, the hunger for connection, for significance, the need for love. And if we can find it in ourselves to offer those things, strangers open up like flowers in sunlight, and jungles become gardens.

What I learned today #316

Self-punishment helps no-one. We can hold ourselves to account without our high standards becoming cruel cages. No more starving or stuffing, no more daily self-destruction. If we are not patient and understanding with ourselves, how can we hope to be consistent contributors to a healthier humanity? Let our caring for the world include ourselves.

Rikki Beadle-Blair

What I learned today #317

To raise your hand to another is a painful sacrifice of dignity on both sides. Let's avoid teaching children that the way to get your point across is to push, punch or yell it. Let's resist confirming our opponent's view that the world belongs to the angry and the loud. When we strike let's be sure it's not just the ego reacting, let's be sure it's necessary and effective.

What I learned today #318

It's not about getting healthy, fit or strong – most of us were born that way – it's about halting the damage that's been done ever since. We are in charge of what we do and what we eat, drink and think, and as we gather the years it's not the breakdown of our body that needs to concern us, but the breakdown of our spirit. Nothing is more fatal than a faltering heart.

Rikki Beadle-Blair

What I learned today #319

It's not easy to witness those we love making obvious mistakes. But sometimes it's crucial. Yes, it's our duty to point to the disaster on the horizon - but then we have to respect their choice not to take our word for it and let them ride out the storm. Learning to watch Baby fall while appreciating the spectacle of Baby taking his or her first step can be a magic moment of growth for everyone.

What I learned today #320

You lose nothing with the passing of time, you only gain. Your never deteriorate, you merely evolve. Death and loss are simply our frightened names for change, which is eternal, inescapable and beautiful, and we need never dread or resist it. We can in fact explore it and carve out new routes for others to follow. We can be a testament to this wild adventure. We can be pioneers.

Rikki Beadle-Blair

What I learned today #321

Confidence is all. Without self-belief, we are defeated at kick-off. It's crucial to talk to those we care about every day - including ourselves - and remind these skittish spirits that we believe in them – that we appreciate their strengths, admire their ambition and can see so clearly just how fabulous they are. Let's be team-mates, coaches, cheerleaders and fans, let's be star-makers, let's be friends.

What I learned today #322

No one can make you feel anything. No one else is responsible for your responses, moods or emotions - just you. How you're affected by others is governed by your expectations and whether they're being met. When we stop demanding anything of the world, we liberate ourselves from the tyranny of need and find our pockets full of gifts. When we own our feelings we free the angry slave inside.

Rikki Beadle-Blair

What I learned today #323

You can't make the most of what's around you until you've made the most of what's within you. To go forward first go within. Once your heart and mind are aligned your body will be too. When your spirit achieves peace you'll bring serenity to the party to share with us all. Calm the chaos, clear your mind and you clear the way forward. For everyone.

What I learned today #324

You get out of the world what you put into it, and same goes for your body. If you want your body to be kind and loyal, you need to be loving and sensitive with it, listen to it, love it and insist on the best. If you want premium performance, then use premium fuel. Test it, stretch it, but don't bully your body, don't insult, abuse or neglect it. Appreciate it. Appreciate yourself.

Rikki Beadle-Blair

What I learned today #325

A day spent doing what you love is more than a day spent in Heaven; it's a day truly spent on Earth. People who talk about living in the 'real world' are rarely living life to the full. Whenever you're feeling lost, watch out for the moments when the raw, unrefined part of yourself comes alive - then discard excuses, push aside distractions and set off in pursuit of yourself.

What I learned today #326

Connection is food and there is famine. People are looking for someone who is pleased to see them. Say hello to someone new. Pay a compliment to someone you see often. Share what you have and watch it multiply. People are the best investment. Save a little bit of everyone; take an interest. Measure your wealth in time given and shared and live like a king of hearts.

Rikki Beadle-Blair

What I learned today #327

Why not show respect to all people, including those in dark circumstances: homeless, addicted, 'unproductive'. Whether you choose to give money or not, give food or not, or give advice or not - whether others choose to be on the streets or not - we can still make our own choice to approach them as equals. Humanity costs nothing. We can afford to give it away. To everyone.

What I learned today #328

If you're lost, take a moment, be where you are, decide where you want to go and take a step. If you're exhausted, rest, take a breath - take a step. If you're afraid, be bold, be brave - take a step. If you're sure in your core that you want to go forward, take a step forward with all your heart. You can't get anywhere if you don't make a move. Take a step. Take another.

Rikki Beadle-Blair

What I learned today #329

When it comes to career, nothing beats a simple strong solid work ethic. When things fall apart, you'll always know how to restart. When inspiration fails and pro-misers desert you, you have what it takes to make something happen. The good news is: when it's in pursuit of your passion, it doesn't feel like work, it just feels like you're doing the right thing. No work – just ethics.

What I've learned today #330

If you want to improve your exterior world, first work on your interior. Your home is a reflection of your spirit, your face a reflection of your mind, your situa-tion a reflection of your attitude. If you want progress, think progressively, if you want love, think lovingly. Serenity and dynamism are states of mind – change your mind and you change your life.

Rikki Beadle-Blair

What I learned today #331

Don't be afraid to want what you want. Own your desires without shame and transform them into determinations. Your life doesn't need to be what happens to other people while you're waiting for perfect weather. Your life can be you acting on the simple decision to fulfil your potential. Your life is you happening. Your life is you living. Your life is yours.

What I learned today #332

Wisdom is maintaining a series of balances: between patience and progress, satisfaction and improvement, understanding and enabling. Wisdom is knowing when to encourage and when to demand, when to turn a blind eye and when to draw the line, when to be direct and when to be sensitive – with others and yourself. Wisdom is knowing when to hold on and when to let go.

Rikki Beadle-Blair

What I learned today #333

Commit. Never let it be said that you pursued your passions halfway. Life is about engagement – inhaling deep, filling your lungs, diving in, staying the course, going the distance. If you're not prepared to go for gold, get out of the game and find something that consumes you. Don't look for what you think will impress others or what they will accept – seek out what makes you FEEL. And commit.

What I learned today #334

Complacency is a killer. Never take life or love for granted. Never kid yourself that the journey is complete – when it feels like you're cruising, you are going downhill. Stay fit, stay fresh, stay on course and – if you can keep exploring ways to find satisfaction in sharpening the saw – you will have the keys to the kingdom. But to enjoy the view from the castle – you need to stay awake.

Rikki Beadle-Blair

What I learned today #335

Why worry about life after death when we have life after life? Reborn every morning – every heartbeat calling us to action – urging us on: 'Live, Live, Live.' When the choices seem too many or too few, when satisfaction seems impossible and we simply don't know what to do – all we need to do is live. Live entirely - every perplexing second of everything. Live Live Live.

What I learned today #336

So often we build castles with moats and demand that others earn the right to enter: "Pursue me, Convince me, Deserve me", turning love into a trial, because we don't believe that loving us should or even could be, easy. Relax, get out of your own way and admit that loving you is the most natural thing in the world, and let the ones that love you... simply love you.

Rikki Beadle-Blair

What I learned today #337

There is more to life than winning. So much to gain beyond mere scores and petty victories. Having the last word is rarely as great a result as learning something. Sack that accountant in the brain that's keeping tally of every exchange and looking for deficits. A crucial rule of success is, 'Never be the smartest one in the room.' If you ever are - change rooms.

What I learned today #338

Grievances are cancerous. Every held resentment is a parasite in the mind, consuming energy so badly needed for this odyssey. Put down the weight of dead moments and make space in your arms for health and happiness. Why carry the burden of other's mistakes? Are you ready to admit there is so much more to you than your sad story? We move so much faster when we stop carrying grudges.

Rikki Beadle-Blair

What I learned today #339

Sometimes you have to let love in, sometimes you have to let love out. Like a semi-wild thing, it can get spooked and run from the house in the dark, or become oddly agoraphobic and too housebound to venture out. Love needs exercise to keep healthy. Love needs coaxing to keep it brave. Love needs a combination of attention and freedom – like every other living thing. Let love run, let love live.

What I learned today #340

We want the best for loved ones. When they're trapped, addicted or lost, we offer advice, money and manipulation to try and change them. But what would happen if we just loved them exactly as they are before expecting anything else? Who might they become then? One who is truly loved without demands? Now that's change. Who might we be? One who loves without pressure? Change indeed.

Rikki Beadle-Blair

What I learned today #341

Almost every advance you make will be through the people you know (or more accurately, the people who know you). Sounds unfair? Well, anyone can make friends and that's basically all there is to the art of Networking: saying hello and making friends. Never take friends for granted. Never use or alienate others. However well you're doing, you will always need true friends... treasure them.

What I learned today #342

The only rejection that matters is the rejection of self; the only acceptance that counts is self-acceptance. We can all learn from one another, but when we slip into self-hatred and channel resources into wishing we were someone else, we start to withhold and swindle the world. Stop resisting our diversity, offer your treasure and get on with the job of being beautiful. Your contribution is needed.

Rikki Beadle-Blair

What I learned today #343

There is such a thing as a chosen one, who wields ultimate power over your destiny. And you choose them. You choose to trust them, to follow them, support them, depend on them. Choose yourself. Whatever else you believe in – believe in yourself. Your power over your destiny is so vast that it's hard to grasp, but it's real. The vehicle is moving, choose to seize the wheel and drive.

What I learned today #344

Do the right thing. When you're unsure or overwhelmed, if integrity is your habit, integrity will guide you. Be as truthful as you can, as tactful as you can manage. Do right by everyone – friend or foe – and you might not get the quick bucks and you may not win the short game, but you will always know where, what and who you are. That's the game to win... and you're the prize.

Rikki Beadle-Blair

What I learned today #345

If you want to transform this world – you can. We are all fractals of the world around us – the micro that shapes the macro. However tiny, we are each of us mighty. For the change to begin, you only have to change one thing: yourself. So start the revolution with the only person you have the right to control: Show us, teach us, inspire us. Be mighty.

What I learned today #346

If you feel like giving up... give up. Give up fretting, give up struggling, let go of feeling cheated because others don't run to your schedule, drop the fear and frustration, stop accumulating disappointment. Perhaps it's not easy but it is this simple: Life is only as much fun as you are. Shrug off excess suffering, say 'So what?', ask yourself 'Now what?' and start the next adventure.

Rikki Beadle-Blair

What I learned today #347

Worrying about what people think of you will only paralyse you. If you live the right way, the world will know. It'll be there in your eyes, your voice, in the way you move. People may be thrown or fearful, but they will know. And if they take time to catch up, in the meantime you will know. Van Gogh sold no paintings, but he had a house of Van Goghs. Let your house be filled with you.

What I learned today #348

In a world crammed with awkward people, the first thing is to get comfortable. Learn to be at home in your skin, in any circumstance. It's a relief to finally let anxiety subside; to relax your racing mind and let your body flow. Allow yourself to feel welcome in the world and offer opportunities and inspiration for others to feel as equally at ease with you as you are with yourself.

Rikki Beadle-Blair

What I learned today #349

You are the universe – your experience of existence. You're the landscape and the weather. You decide if it's a good day or if you're wasting time; you can kill the vibe or start the party; you decree if you are lovable. If there is an enemy – it's you. Deceivers? All you. Whenever there's a problem it's you – and you are the solution. You're everything from the epic to the incidental. You are God.

What I learned today #350

Nothing ages you faster than worrying about wrinkles. Nothing makes you uglier than constantly staring in the mirror. If you fret about weight, all you'll think about is food. No one falls in love with their stalker. Grip the soap too hard and it slips away. Desperation is unattractive. Fear is unappealing. Stop scaring fortune away and get on with being blessed. It's so much more fun.

Rikki Beadle-Blair

What I learned today #351

The better the excuses the worse the career, the slower the progress, the sadder the story. Stop turning your loved ones into alibis. Stop betraying your body with blame, stop rewriting opportunity as tragic biography. There is one reason and one reason only - that reason is you. Stop designing a life out of Why Nots, and use that creativity to take back this day. No excuses, no delay.

What I learned today #352

The secret to wisdom and eternal youth are the same - a boundless curiosity. Nothing is more attractive than an enquiring mind. Take interest in the world and you will never be lost for fresh ideas. A miracle waits within everything, no matter how grey and uninspiring it seems. Everyone you meet is a potential adventure; life is a playground full of inspirational new friends. Say hello.

Rikki Beadle-Blair

What I learned today #353

Everyone deserves a love song. Something created specially for them: a poem, a book, an email, a note attached to roses. Somewhere someone is wondering if you ever think of them, tragically unaware of your depth of feeling. Perhaps you are best friends, perhaps you are family, perhaps you're married to them. Every kind of love craves expression. Don't hold back, serenade someone.

What I learned today #354

If you crawl reluctantly out of the sheets, craving coffee, resenting the day ahead and leave the house starving, what kind of day have you begun? It's time to open your eyes, let the light in, nourish yourself. Are you ready to dig into the day and see what's it's holding for you? This morning are you ready to rise?

Rikki Beadle-Blair

What I learned today #355

The course of your life is decided by the quality of your thinking. Think small and options shrink, devalue yourself and life becomes cheap, decide you're unlucky and opportunity will agree. Stop constructing your circumstances out of limited beliefs. Stop investing in reasons to not be yourself. Forget thinking outside the box - break the box up and burn it. Think bold. Think big.

What I learned today #356

When you have a problem, make sure it really is one. Is this just not what you expected? Is this your chance for something unexpected? Is this a signal to try something new? A cue to show what you're really made of? Is this what you really need? Look again - sometimes the problem is that you're reluctant to do what's required. Sometimes the problem is that there is no problem.

Rikki Beadle-Blair

What I learned today #357

There is no better version of you available elsewhere. If you're being the best you can be and someone does not want you, then they want someone else entirely and you're free. No need to take another's requirements as a judgement. Let them get on with their search for happiness while you get on with yours. You won't find validation in the eyes of those who don't get you. Focus on those who do.

What I learned today #358

Treat yourself to an honest conversation with your life. Your body is telling you if you're caught in destructive patterns. Your partners and peers are telling you when your standards are too low. Your spirit is telling you whether your life is on course. If something's been bothering you for ages, perhaps it's time for a different approach. Life is talking to you. The trick is to listen.

Rikki Beadle-Blair

What I learned today #359

We are only using a tiny percentage of our brains at any given moment - left to wonder what could be achieved if we used 100%. But would we do if we used 100% of our common sense, our application, creativity, ambition or humanity? What if we embraced every second? Who would we be if we committed to life without restraint? Superhuman? Or just entirely beautifully human?

What I learned today #360

Safety is not always in numbers. Just because it's the done thing doesn't mean it needs to be done again. An independent mind is not a betrayal of your ancestors. It doesn't serve society to leave it unquestioned. Thank your elders for the experience they offer, but gracefully decline to be a clone. Pay tribute to past pioneers, customize their wisdom, respect your elders - and rebel.

Rikki Beadle-Blair

What I learned today #361

We create enemies as alibis for the life we are holding back from. We tell ourselves, "Why should I be perfect when others aren't?" and, "How can I be positive when there are demons in the world?" We dodge happiness and postpone progress in the name of grievance and rage, but perhaps what we really feel is jealousy - the convoluted desire to be our enemy, when true satisfaction lies in making peace with ourselves.

What I learned today #362

Success is entirely in your hands. You decide what it is. You decide if you deserve it. You decide if you are capable of it. You decide if it's worth the effort. You decide if you've achieved it. You decide whether to accept it. You decide whether to enjoy it. You decide whether to share it. You were born a success. You will die one. What kind of success is up to you. It's all up to you.

Rikki Beadle-Blair

What I learned today #363

Until you have tried everything - given everything - expect nothing. The more you want the more you must offer - anything less is a beg or a swindle. Be honest with yourself and you will find your scared, spoilt, lazy, deluded self behind every misfire, and your passion, preparation and persistence at the spark of every breakthrough. This is how your life works - it works as hard as you do.

What I learned today #364

Other's fortune is not your misfortune. Born wealthier than you? More popular? Believe it or not, someone somewhere envies your wealth and popularity. Stop comparing and start celebrating all blessings everywhere. No life suits you better than the one you have and no other is available. You wouldn't want to swap problems with anyone. Don't ask to be lucky. Make everyone you meet feel lucky. That's success.

Rikki Beadle-Blair

What I learned today #365

Every day teaches something new - if you're willing to learn. And this year has taught me, it all basically comes down to the same thing: You create Heaven and Hell. Hell hides in making others responsible for your story, Heaven lies in full honest ownership of your life. No one else can make you happy, beautiful, desirable or valuable. You are all your problems and solutions. You have total power. And you can choose to use it wisely.

Whew! The final 'What I learned today.' It's been my nightly meditation and my daily mantra, and through all the amazing responses, encouragements, debates and challenges I have grown more than I could ever have imagined possible. And reading them back, what I ultimately learn is that every stumble is still a step - the trick is to stumble with grace. And whatever happens to me, I deserve the lesson. Because learning is life. And I love it.

Rikki Beadle-Blair

Lightning Source UK Ltd.
Milton Keynes UK
UKOW051803240112

186001UK00001B/10/P